The Smugglers of the Sulu Islands
A Travel Memoir

Ken Jackson

Caynham House Press—Birmingham, AL
ISBN: 979-8-218-14740-2
Library of Congress Control Number: 2023901806
The Smugglers of the Sulu Islands: A Travel Memoir
Author: Ken Jackson
Digital distribution | 2023
Paperback | 2023

For Aly

Who got me into the Sulu Islands, and who was
prepared to leave me there

Buy the ticket, take the ride.

Hunter S. Thompson

Introduction

Many of the stories in this collection were written from around 1985 until 2005, when I lived in Hong Kong and traveled throughout Asia. The rest were written while I wandered around during my retirement. As such, they won't be useful guides for selecting restaurants and bars (with some exceptions) or hotels (with no exceptions).

They are simply a record of where I went, how I got there (and in a few cases, how I got out of there), who I met, and what I felt about those places and people and ultimately myself.

I have prefaced several of the stories with some historical context. For example, trips to West Belfast, and East Timor, and especially to the Khyber Pass, would be different now. On the other hand, a tour of a Mexican border town with a beer drinking taxi driver, a cruise through the Caribbean on a gravel barge, and a Calcutta cricket match riot are timeless travel experiences.

The stories aren't so much organized as they are loosely clumped into geographical groups: Southeast Asia, India and Pakistan, Island Nations, Europe, America, and Hong Kong, Taiwan, Macau.

KJ

Southeast Asia

Chapter One
The Smugglers of the Sulu Islands

If you don't count the time it takes to buy a ticket, the fastest way to Tawi Tawi, the last major Philippine island in the Sulu chain, is to fly from Zamboanga. If you do count the time it takes to buy a ticket, swimming comes out about the same.

Not understanding this simple principle, my wife and I walked into Zamboanga's Philippine Airline ticket office, took number 183, and sat down in the back of a crowded waiting room. A display indicated that number 14 was being served. An hour passed. Number 14 was still being served—or not—because all that seemed to be happening was bulk sales of tickets to travel agents who walked up to the counters without taking a number and spent lots of time and money.

Amazingly, customers holding numbers 15-182 seemed placid; resigned to the inherent injustice of this system. Or perhaps they just needed a place to sit out of the blazing sun for a few hours and had no travel plans at all. In either case the only two people who seemed bothered by the professional queue jumpers were me and the other foreigner sitting next to me. Our responses were different. I went out to look for a travel agent to jump the queue on my behalf to the detriment of numbers 15 et seq.

When I returned without one, siesta having intervened, my wife had vanished. Assuming she'd been kidnapped by one of the competing liberation armies, I began rehearsing my explanation to her mother. I'd reached the part about bargaining for a discount on the ransom when she suddenly emerged from the private manager's office behind the ticket counter. She was bitterly complaining to the station chief about blatant and presumably reciprocal favoritism between travel agents and ticket sellers at her expense.

After a few minutes open and honest exchange of views on the subject the manager threw up his hands and said: "Where do you want to go, Madam?" Then, without a trace of irony, he added: "And how soon can you leave?" I don't know if he meant how soon could she leave Zamboanga, the Philippines, that office, or just his life, but sooner was clearly better than later.

Luckily for everyone concerned, sooner was the case. We caught a flight an hour later to the last airport at the edge of the Sulu islands. Thirty minutes after that we bounced down on a small landing strip surrounded by military jeeps, tanks, and guys in camouflage with really long machine guns—and those were the good guys! The bad guys were on the next island. They thought the government of the Sulus should return to its ethnic roots and were happy to fire random mortar rounds into the villages to punctuate their opinion.

The airstrip was a short jeepney ride from the metropolis of Bongao, the capital of Tawi Tawi. We were expecting, after the difficulty of getting there, to find a sleepy pristine provincial community. We found a nonstop motorcycle rally down a dusty main street. Small clapboard and pre-form shop houses fronted the street. Beyond it was a frenetic harbor jammed with narrow wooden boats. The harbor served as transport depot, public warehouse, and live fish market.

The town itself had a Malay feel about it. Stilted kampong fishing villages crowded the water's edge, while inland, local Society lived in sturdy tile roofed bungalows set in shady tropical gardens. Scattered throughout the surrounding palm forests were small concrete-block mosques topped with green corrugated steel domes.

The tourist industry hadn't fully developed in Tawi Tawi. The only accommodation we could find, the Southern Hotel, was on the second floor above a grain storage facility. The guidebook's description of it set a new standard for the word "Basic." The bath was not "en suite." It was not even "en hotel." The toilet could have featured in the Journal of Entomology: "Enormous Green Cockroaches Discovered!"

The most interesting aspects of the hotel were the spray-painted graffiti on the bedroom walls and the fact that the only door to the building was pad locked from the outside at night. But it did have two large balconies. They looked out the back over a lagoon instead of onto the Grand Prix training ground in front and offered some relief from the noise and fumes.

After freshening up in our new quarters, we decided to explore. Primarily, we decided to explore the possibility of different quarters. We eventually gave up on this fool's errand when we happily stumbled upon a pleasant looking open-air bamboo and thatch bar on a small palm fringed cove.

Yes, Lord....

For reasons that will be apparent we came to call this place the "Smuggler's Bar" and it became our refuge from the Southern Hotel. The Smuggler's was packed at 1:00 p.m. the day we found it. Judging from the number of empty San Miguel bottles stacked on the tables and spilled onto the floor and out into the road, it had apparently been packed for hours.

It was filled with local fishing types and soldiers from the nearby base. There were only a few guns in view, but almost everyone wore a knife. We had no trouble making the immediate life-long friends one might expect when a tall blonde female and a guy willing to buy drinks walk into such an environment. The most friendly person was a tall good-looking soldier named Sgt. Ali. He decided right off that my wife would enjoy a long ride on the back of his motorcycle. Maybe it was his honest good looks, or maybe it was just his M16, but neither of us really saw a problem with the idea.

During her prolonged absence, I discovered The Smuggler's had a kitchen. It specialized in two types of haute cuisine—Maggi Instant Noodles With Egg and Maggi Instant Noodles Without Egg ("Egg Maggi" and "Plain Maggi" to the initiated). There was also an old tape deck but whatever it was trying to play was drowned out by the free-flowing discourse in ideas among the patrons.

After several hours of pleasantries, everyone at our table except Sgt. Ali announced they had to take a boat that night to the Malaysian state of Sabah, on Borneo, where they would be working on a forestry project for two weeks. They all stood up, more or less in unison, leaned toward the beach and disappeared. A few minutes later we saw them streaking across the water in an open boat powered by four massive Evinrude engines. Hunched into the wind, wearing balaclavas, they pitched brown glass ballast into the sea as they surged by.

By then it was nearly dark and our tri-shaw driver had been waiting for almost five hours. So, we returned to the bright lights of Bongao where we discovered a small restaurant that would grill our market fish and throw in a plate of rice and a bowl of Maggi for a dollar. We never ate anywhere else.

The next morning, after being released from the Southern, we went off in search of a sightseeing boat. Initially, we wanted to find one to take us to the last island in the Philippines--Sitangkai. Sitangkai is another of those "Venice of the Easts" that guidebook writers seem to locate everywhere. After sitting on rice bags at the local congressman's warehouse drinking tea and interviewing boatmen for an hour, we determined no available boat was fast enough to make a day trip to this place that had even less accommodation selection than Bongao. We settled for a boat tour of the nearby Bajao tribal areas.

The Bajao are often called Sea Gypsies. They are traditional nomadic fishermen who follow an animistic faith. Their sacred spots are small spits of sand within a few kilometers of Bongao harbour. Out past a small island shaped like a chicken head named "Chicken Head Island" in the local language, we found some of them. These tiny islands lie in very shallow pale blue water. They are windswept and eerily tranquil. The Bajao erect sticks around them to fly ripped up bits of blue and white cloth. In the otherwise total silence of these small isolated blindingly white places, the incessant flapping of those rough flags does seem spiritual. Anyone who has seen Buddhist prayer flags among the snowy outposts of the Himalaya would recall that simple serenity.

The Bajao, unfortunately have a downside, too. They are nomadic fishermen with access to explosives. The mounds of sun-bleached shattered coral washed up throughout the Sulus all the way to Zamboanga testify to the destructive consequences of this combination. We saw a few Bajao in their long wooden boats with squid and octopus drying from the stern. They seemed friendly and as carefree as anyone who doesn't yet worry about living near a dynamited coral reef.

With that depressing thought, we returned to The Smuggler's and discovered to our amazement that the "forestry" boat gang had returned and were sitting in exactly the same spot they been had a day earlier with at least as many empties around. They had made the 150 km sea journey without collecting even a trace of sawdust. I might be pretty naive, but it didn't take much to guess that these guys had nothing to do with trees. They were in the "Duty Free Shopping Business."

This looked to me like the answer to the day trip to Sitangkai. It was half the distance they'd just traveled, and I could pay enough. So, we started talking about the boat and how fast it was and eventually I asked the potentially fatally moronic question: "Where is it moored?" At this a man with a scarf around his head and a world class facial scar came up from another table, sat down and quietly said: "My friend, I do not mind if you sit here. I do not even mind if you drink with us and talk with us. But, my friend, if you mention the boat again, I will hurt you."

Well, that sort of thing can be a real conversation stopper. I decided to change subjects while my wife decided to change tables and renew a meaningful friendship with Sgt Ali as far away from me as possible. We eventually backed out of The Smuggler's, found our tri-shaw driver and returned to the comfort of our pad locked hotel.

The next morning, my wife began our last full day in Tawi Tawi by asking me that timeless travel question; "Okay you Jerk, Where's the fucking beach?" It was true we hadn't really seen one, so we flagged down the first tri-shaw driver to whom she repeated her query. He thought Boracay might be the nearest, but sensing a volatile situation, he took us to a spot that had somehow escaped our notice. Beyond a mangrove was a desolate sheltered curve of white sand with overhanging banyans and water so clear Evian might try to bottle it. Schools of fish glistened in florescent colour. And there were no people...no people...no people....

We'd found the bath the Southern had forgot and we soaked and we swam until Happy Hour at The Smuggler's—which for me meant after "My Special Friend" had left for Borneo.

Nightfall brought us back to the grilled fish restaurant for our farewell dinner. Stuffed on seabass and still lingering over beers, we were approached by a man I suddenly realized I had seen before. With no invitation, he sat down and said, "I understand you are flying back to Zamboanga tomorrow. I hope you had a nice stay. I'll walk you to your hotel now. The army assigned me to make sure you had no trouble here. I almost failed yesterday when you mentioned the boat."

Walking back, we saw Sgt. Ali for the last time. He was listing slightly in the middle of the road with his machine gun, a full bandolero, a vacant smile and a distant stare. Thankfully, his motorcycle was elsewhere.

Chapter Two
An American in Dalat
(Before Americans Were Allowed in Dalat)

"Welcome to Dalat. Please give me your passports. You are American? How do you come here?"

Not an unusual greeting from the young female receptionist in a white "ao dai" local dress at the Dalat Palace Hotel, my traveling companion and I thought. But this was 1988 and there were still some leftover issues between the Vietnamese and Americans. Especially between the Vietnamese and some American war veterans who had recently snuck into the area to arm a post-war insurgency.

Not realizing this political nuance and exhausted from the drive up from Saigon battling the revenge of the half-cooked shrimp, we replied, "We came up by car. That's our driver over there. He's the skinny chain-smoking guy who looks really sad to be working over Tet."

"No," our receptionist persisted, "I do not ask how you arrive here. I ask how you are American and you are in Dalat? Dalat is forbidden for Americans. You must leave now. The police will come tonight to collect all foreign passports. They will see yours. You will be arrested. No one can help you."

Then she asked for our, at that time mandatory, travel permits which our driver's travel agency prepared for us. Saigon-Dalat-Nha Trang-Saigon it said in English. But, of course, as we learned from her, the official, Nothing-Else-Counts, Vietnamese version was slightly different...No Dalat.

At this point, she switched to Vietnamese and shouted at our cowering driver. We guessed she was questioning his morality and even his sanity for illegally bringing Americans to the forbidden place (even for cash dollars), and she was demanding that he take over the problem and solve it immediately.

It didn't matter. We were cooked. Any more time in that car and at the roadside latrines would have surely killed us quicker than a Dalat jail, and we told her we could not leave. She was silent for a few moments. Then with a Gallic-Oriental shrug, and a final brief warning about the hopelessness of our fate, she registered us into the hotel.

So, what do you do on your last night of Dalat freedom? You go to the Dalat Fair! Everyone in the town was there. The fair wasn't very up-market. The Texas State Fair had nothing to worry about. But it did have some special diversions for two--soon to be incarcerated--travellers.

First, there were lots of animals. The animals weren't actually exhibits. They just wandered up from the countryside to see what all the lights and noise were about.

There were also rides. The few rides that were working seemed to have been cobbled together from spare parts abandoned by the advancing armies of Genghis Khan. To paraphrase a line from

"Apocalypse Now" (and many such lines were flashing through my head that night): "If you will get on one of these rides, you will never have to prove your courage in any other way." We left the rides alone.

But most importantly, there were the games of chance. My friend and I won a warm, dusty liter bottle of Dalat Beer by throwing a rubber ring over the bottle's neck. An accommodating Carnie ripped off the rusty bottle cap for us with an even rustier machete and a few sour gulps confirmed that second prize was surely two liters of Dalat Beer.

The locals weren't very interested in the beer game. But an excited crowd, surging around a large circular table, shouted, cursed and waved wads of grubby Dong at each other. When we eventually elbowed our way close, we discovered that the table was surrounded by 40 tiny, numbered compartments that looked like miniature doghouses.

In the center of the table was an upside-down circular plastic container that looked like (and probably was) a cake cover. The cake cover was attached to a string. The string ran up through a pulley and down into the hand of a guy who was exchanging numbered tickets for Dong. The ticket numbers corresponded to the numbers on the tiny doghouses. When the String Holder sold all his tickets, he pulled down the string to raise the cake cover and release a really startled rat.

The rat stood motionless for an instant before he realized that there were dozens of screaming humans within grabbing distance of him. Then he bolted. He sprinted two quick laps around the table and dove for refuge into a numbered dog/rat house. The winning ticket was paid. The rat was retrieved and returned to the cake cover. The betting resumed.

Upon learning that each Rat Roulette ticket cost about four American cents, my friend and I bought all the tickets for the next round and handed them out to our new Dalat friends. You never know when you might need someone to bring you a dusty bottle of warm beer while you're sitting in the stir waiting for Henry Kissinger to negotiate your release at the next Paris Peace Conference.

The Fair shut early. The generators pooped out. We returned to the Palace Hotel to await our forthcoming legal entanglements. Nothing happened that night. We just grabbed another warm beer from our non-working frig, sat on our balcony overlooking the dismantled remnants of the Dalat Fair and wondered how bad tomorrow would be when the police arrived.

Morning came with its furry-mouthed, alcohol-induced headache regrets. But despite that, we had to face our fate. We went down to the lobby expecting to be handcuffed and hauled away. But no police lurked in the lobby. Our receptionist from the previous night again commanded her desk.

When she saw us, she drew us aside and quietly said: "Do you remember the bus of French tourists who arrived yesterday? I put all of their passports on top of your passports before I gave them to the police. And the police, maybe they were a little tired, or maybe they were a little lazy, but they did not search every passport, and they did not find your illegal American passports."

We were holding our breath when she said, "I should have told the police about you when they came here. I regret I did not tell them, because it was my duty. Tomorrow the police will come again. And tomorrow," she paused, "you will not be so lucky."

We didn't need to be lucky tomorrow. We were lucky enough today. We rounded up our miserable driver, who cranked up the engine of our ancient Citroen, and lurched off toward Nha Trang.

Today, Dalat is a major Southeast Asia tourist destination. The Palace Hotel has returned to, and perhaps exceeded, its French colonial grandeur. It is now a true luxury hotel with air conditioning instead of languid overhead fans; with Internet access instead of Bakelite telephones of purely decorative purpose; with fully stocked mini bars instead of enamelled storage boxes unconnected to electricity. Where the Dalat Fair once entertained local farmers, a football stadium is now under construction.

A quarter century ago, during Vietnam's emergence from decades of calamitous war, Dalat was just a mountain way station with an agreeable climate and lots of flowers. Its people were poor enough to want to stake pennies on the whims of a frightened rodent. But they were also rich enough to pardon two hapless travellers through an unsolicited, if slightly reluctant, act of kindness.

Chapter Three
A Saigon Shopping Spree

"So, you're going to Vietnam? Can you pick up an 'ao dai' for me while you're there?" If a casual female friend ever says this to you, politely decline. Say you're sorry; you'll be too busy. Say anything, but do not agree to do it unless you want to reduce your squad of casual female friends.

Ao dais (pronounced "ow dzai" in the north and "ow yai" in the south) are form-fitted, calf length shirts worn over blousy pants. High-necked and long-sleeved, the shirt snaps down both sides for ventilation adjustments that reveal a triangle of midriff at certain angles. They are usually made from silk or a silky synthetic.

Almost every woman and girl in the south wore them until the communists from the north took over in 1975. Afterwards they went a little out of fashion as a bourgeois affectation. Happily, for their male fans, they have made a big comeback. Schoolgirls always wore them, but now they are quite normal dress again. At lunch hour in Saigon, the downtown streets are clogged with ao-daied cyclists. At night, you're welcomed into restaurants, cafes and even billiard halls by ao-daied staff.

Perhaps no other article of traditional Asian national dress exposes so little yet reveals so much. This phenomenon is due to two important features. First, the fabric is translucent in the stark tropical sunlight. Second, the tops appear to be painted on. One size certainly does not fit all.

Surprisingly, women who wear them don't seem to suffer from restricted movement. They can easily maneuver motor scooters through crowded streets. I even saw one young woman shooting pool in the southern town of Vung Tau run a table off the break while wearing a tight ao dai and counting my money. She had close-cropped hair, which is unusual for Vietnamese, and I asked her why she cut it so short. "Hard enough shooting pool in ao dai without hair in face, too," she explained, as she potted another ball and counted some more of my money.

Ao dais are comfortable, but sensual. It's the sensual aspect that causes difficulty in buying one for a casual friend. My crisis started innocently enough during a break between two business meetings.

"Is there anything you'd like to see or do?" my local host Tran asked.

I could have said, "I'd like to take a nap," or, "I'd like to munch a snake bile baguette," or, "I'd like see how long I can stand in the middle of Dong Khoi Street before a motorcycle hits me." But no. I had to say, "I'd like to buy an ao dai for a friend."

Vietnamese hosts are nothing if not helpful and efficient, and my buddy Tran was no exception. I had no sooner spoken these ill-conceived words than he was shouting into his mobile phone to his wife for a recommendation. Of course, a "deluxe, only the best for my American pal" recommendation was given, and off we went.

We shortly arrived at a small shop sandwiched between a noodle stall and a bicycle repair stand. The front of the shop offered simple souvenirs, like stuffed cobras, Ho Chi Minh T-shirts, and war surplus Zippo lighters. Beyond this section, through a curtain, was the ao dai center. My first surprise was that there were no ao dais for sale. I was expecting racks of them—ready to wear. My friend had told me her height and weight. I thought I could eyeball a fit.

It quickly became apparent, after an extravagant greeting by the owner, who'd been alerted by Madame Tran, that this wasn't a dress shop. It was a tailor shop. It produced formal, silk embroidered, "suitable for the Bastille Day Ball at the French Embassy" ao dais. And that is precisely what they were prepared to do for my unsuspecting pre-former casual friend. And they were going to do it as a very special order—ready the next morning.

After the obligatory tea ceremony, we got down to the serious business of selecting a style and taking down measurements with Tran interpreting. Style was easy. It was all in her order: "plain white top, plain white pants. No birds or flowers in luxuriant pastel stitching. Just plain white."

Then, the owner produced a drawing of a female form with places to write the measurements of some very personal body parts. Armed only with height and weight and never having seen my friend in anything besides conservative office clothes, I had a problem. Everyone tried to be helpful, especially Tran, who began to sense my predicament.

"She's fairly thin. Maybe a 24-inch waist. I have no idea about her hip size."

Don't worry, they assured me, "the shirt is open on the sides below the waist. You can make a small mistake on the hip size. It won't matter. But the bust is crucial. You can't make any mistake on the bust size or the ao dai will be—well—a bust."

The ensuing conversation between Tran and me went: "But I have no clue."

"You must make your best guess. Is she big or small?"

"Medium, I suppose."

Tran translated and then spent some additional time with a quizzical look on his face listening to the women before he turned back to me and reported: "I'm afraid that to make the ao dai, they must know the exact size of your friend's breasts."

In despair and growing frustration that I couldn't leave and forget the whole, by now, absurd and humiliating scene, I told Tran I had no idea about the particulars of my friend's torso because I had never seen her naked. She was, after all, just a friend! Tran put this message into Vietnamese. After a pause to absorb this new fact, one woman said something and the rest of them began to grin. The grins turned into those hand-over-the-mouth Asian giggles. The giggles dissolved into those deep belly laughs that render you bent over and teary-eyed and gasping for air when you finally recover.

Tran tried unsuccessfully to remain aloof from the hilarity. He took moment to calm himself before he turned back, still slightly smiling, and said, "It seems very odd to them. You have never seen this woman's body. She is not your wife or your lover. So, why on Earth do you want to buy an ao dai for her?"

The women had a point. Victoria's Secret sells less intimate apparel. I gave up. I told Tran they'd just have to do their best. But I wasn't getting off that easy. The entire staff, including seamstresses, was now being marshaled toward the front of the shop where I was supposed to walk past, like a military inspection, to pick the girl whose shape was the closest match. Focused on escape, I picked the girl nearest the door, which I immediately jumped through and into Tran's waiting car.

I returned to the shop the next day in a driving tropical rainstorm. I picked up my package, stuffed it into a drenched backpack, left for the airport and flew home. That was when my problems really started.

If you ever do make the mistake of buying an ao dai for a casual female friend, my further advice is: Do not compound your error by regaling her with the story of a roomful of giggling strangers holding out cupped hands trying to help you guess her chest size. Just give her the sack with the certain knowledge that it won't fit, apologize in advance and cut your losses.

I didn't follow this simple tactic. I told her the whole story. I didn't even leave out the "Why are you here if you aren't sleeping with her?" part. She listened in stunned silence, with that classic "I can't believe I'm hearing this, you moron," look on her face. Then with one of those half chuckles that could easily turn into a gag reflex, she took the parcel and left.

I haven't seen her since. But I did have a short one-sided conversation with her to this effect: "I really don't appreciate you talking about my body. The thing didn't fit anyway. You picked the wrong model. The material isn't even real silk. I burned it. It melted. It's plastic. Goodbye."

Um…goodbye.

Chapter Four
The Golden Triangle
Don't Get Off the Boat

In the late 1980's the Golden Triangle border region of Thailand, Burma, and Laos was controlled by ethnic Chinese opium warlords. The warlord regime arose after soldiers of Chang Kai-shek's defeated Nationalist army fled the Communists into Burma at the end of the Chinese Revolution. It developed and thrived under off-books reciprocal arrangements with certain elements of the official militaries. The Golden Triangle's notorious reputation for lawlessness persisted for decades.

Nevertheless, in 1988, my friend, Bob and I got together over a few Singha beers one night and thought: "What a fun place to visit!" We agreed to take a boat up the Kok River into the Triangle from the northern Thai city of Chiang Rai. I figured Bob was a good companion for this outing because he was a Vietnam War combat veteran.

Unfortunately, this was before the advent of sightseeing tour boats, and our time was limited. I decided we should ride upriver toward Laos on a commercial passenger boat and disembark at some midway point to catch a scheduled downriver boat back to Chiang Rai. There were three critical flaws with my plan.

We encountered the first flaw at the wooden shed that served as the departure terminal for the Kok River boat service. There, we discovered that the schedule was written only in Thai, and no one spoke English. The words that appeared to be names of mid-trip destinations, were not followed by arrival times, but only by prices. The price to the last destination was 100 Baht (US$4).

The second flaw was to assume that this pricing system was based upon distances from Chiang Rai. We picked the 40 Baht destination to give ourselves a little margin on half-way, even though we had no idea where or, more importantly, what this place was. We later discovered pricing was not based on distance, but rather, presumably, on some mystical sequence of lucky numbers. The 40 Baht destination turned out to be far beyond half-way, which compounded the impact of the final flaw.

The final and most portentous flaw was to begin our journey at noon. Kok River boat travel was mostly a morning activity. This meant we were unlikely to reach our turn-around point in time to catch the day's last downriver boat back to Chiang Rai.

We knew none of this when we bought our tickets and walked onto the pier. Soon two narrow long-tailed boats pulled up. The first boat, which included a soldier with an M16 rifle, was for Thais. The second, which carried no soldier to equalize the threat from warlord armies and other random criminals, was for foreign tourists. This discrepancy was exacerbated after we shoved off and the soldier's boat quickly left us far behind and soon disappeared from sight.

The ride itself wasn't memorable. The Kok River is shallow and brown, and except for about half a mile of rocky rapids, slow moving. There was very little to look at beyond the jungle-edged shoreline. After about an hour and a half, our helmsman slowed down, eased the boat onto a sandy beach, and gestured at Bob and me to get off. This beach, with no dock, no pier, no shade, no facilities of any kind, and at that moment, no people, was the 40 Baht destination.

We stepped onto land and looked back at our departing riverine lifeline. All the other tourists, who hadn't gotten off the boat, were waving goodbye. A Swedish guy took our photo to include in his album of stupid things he'd seen people do. When our boat engine's drone finally faded away, we were left alone in total silence.

An old wooden hand painted Thai sign hanging askew between two posts probably identified our location, but of course, we still couldn't read Thai. Not far behind us the land rose about 10 feet to a plateau. We climbed up and looked around for a few minutes. Except for a couple of abandoned huts, it was completely barren. Not even a scrawny chicken or a scavenging goat enlivened the scene. We returned to the beach to wait for our ride home.

A driftwood log comprised the beach's only convenience. We sat on it with our single water bottle, ready for the downriver boat to return us to Chiang Rai. Two hours passed. No boat came.

Our initial beach experience was only heat and boredom. As the afternoon wore on, the heat persisted, but when two guys with machetes appeared on the ridge behind us, boredom was no longer a problem. Within minutes the number of machete guys increased a lot. Some of them stood. The rest squatted on the edge of the ridge directly behind us.

There were no women, no children, no pets, just young men with machetes. None of them made a move toward us. Maybe they were too startled by their good fortune. But with sunset approaching, we expected the situation would soon deteriorate.

I try to be an optimistic traveler, but I was having difficulty putting a positive spin on this development. Bob entered a sullen, trance-like state. To cheer him up, I said, "It could be worse. You could be here alone."

Bob looked up and snaped, "If I was alone, I wouldn't be here!"

I left him to his thoughts.

Bob later explained he wasn't in a trance. He was trying to work out a last-stand strategy for us using the river as a defensive perimeter. I still have no idea how that could have worked, but before we had to test it, we heard the distant buzz of a long-tail boat approaching from Chiang Rai.

Bob then implemented a more viable strategy by wading waist deep mid-stream into the river and waving his arms like his life depended on it, which, no doubt it did. Miraculously, the boat was able to stop before plowing him over. One of the Thai passengers shouted: "What the hell are you doing here? Get on the boat before those guys kill you."

Our rescuers turned out to be Thai alumni of the University of Virginia who were headed to a reunion at an upriver lodge. They told us that the 40 Baht destination was, in fact, a prison farm and the armed men behind us were convicts. Someone passed us a bottle of Johnnie Walker Scotch to take the edge off. "Let's give a cheer for dear old UVA!"

When we reached the lodge, we persuaded their boatman to take us back to Chiang Rai for US$100. He took off immediately, and in the quickening twilight, it was not too soon. The driver ordered us to lie flat on the deck to give him a better view of the rocks that would have done us as much damage as the convicts if he had failed to avoid them.

Back in the safety of Chiang Rai, we reflected on our ridiculous, life-threatening day, and we concluded that there is one vital rule to Golden Triangle river travel: Don't Get Off the Boat!

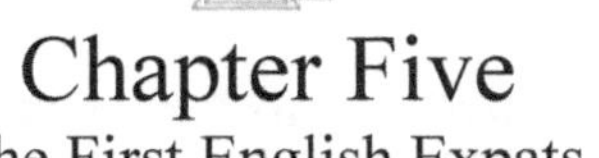

Chapter Five
The First English Expats

In 1603, at a place Europeans then called Bantam, an English fleet trading for spices left behind a few merchants to organize the pepper trade for the arrival of the next voyage—two years later.

These expatriated merchants were known as "factors," a term still used 250 years later at Canton, China. They were completely on their own. Instead of the walled villas with swimming pools and verdant gardens their privileged progeny now enjoy, these original expatriates built primitive wooden structures on the edge of a tidal mud flat. Only two survived to see the next ship.

The factors competed for trade against Indians, Chinese, Arabs, Japanese, Portuguese, and the ubiquitous Dutch. Cutthroat competition was a literal tactic, as were "fire sales" induced by flaming arrows shot into wooden warehouses.

They were plagued with malaria, amoebic dysentery and other tropical diseases. Even if they survived their assignment, they were in almost as much peril on the return voyage from scurvy, piracy and shipwreck. Yet despite the dangers, isolation, and drudgery of life in a hostile swamp, these men and their successors managed to plant the seeds of the Asian expatriate tradition that flourishes today in Jakarta, Bangkok, Manila, Singapore, Hong Kong.

They quickly discovered the consolations of drinking arrack, overeating, and local women. Within a few voyages, the Calvinist captains of the Dutch East India Company were outraged by the rampant "hoares" and drunkards to be found everywhere in Bantam. One English captain threatened to immediately repatriate incorrigible drunks in disgrace--a move that would have decimated the labor pool. Some of them took local wives and refused to return. Their masters back in London constantly accused them of "country trade" (trading for their own account), the 17th century equivalent of voucher fraud.

Admit it. You gotta love these guys. They came with nothing and created a Lifestyle. With this sense of reverence, I decided to visit Banten on a Sunday between meetings in Jakarta. I didn't go to sightsee. My guidebook had warned me that the only sights are a mosque, a fort and some crumbling walls. I didn't care. I was a pilgrim. I wanted to stand on the same mud, sweat under the same sun and be bitten by the same bugs as those ancient expats. I was also hoping some of those "hoares'" descendants might still be around to share a few arracks, but sadly, not even a warm Bintang beer is on offer in this conservative Islamic enclave.

The Bantam those factors knew is difficult to imagine today. Today's backwater fishing village was then the capital of a sultanate. It was as large as contemporary Amsterdam. Now, Banten is easy to reach from Jakarta, but once there, orientation is a little tricky. If you don't hire a guide, you'll spend a long time seeing not much but a narrow street choked with rows of stalls selling religious items, shell jewellery, stuffed animals, dried fruit, and warm soft drinks.

If you arrive on a Sunday, the confusion is increased by activity at the mosque (Mesjid Agung). Thousands come to pray, picnic and queue up to squeeze into the stairwell of a 300-year-old Chinese-style minaret for the best views of the...um... mud flats.

The mosque on a Sunday is a Southeast Asia sensory assault. Blind beggars line the narrow paths of the compound calling for alms. Food is sold and consumed and spilled from dozens of pushcarts. Sanitation aromas ascend from the open drains that crisscross the walk paths.

Near the mosque, Banten's museum offers relief from the chaos and the heat. Its small collection of ceramics, jewellery and weapons, and Hindu carvings are interesting enough. But more importantly, the museum is where I finally found a "guide" who knew the way to the fort, but whose English was limited to, "Mister, I money."

The Dutch built Speelwijk Fort. Its well-kept graveyard recalls the lives of those who didn't repatriate. The fort's interior courtyard is graced by massive tropical hardwoods, and on the day I was there, by children flying kites against the cobalt sky. One watchtower partially remains. Beneath the watchtower, lies a tunnel with small skylights. I thought it might have served as a prison for captured English factors, but "Mister, I money" was not a sufficient exchange of ideas to confirm this.

The fort originally guarded the harbor, but centuries of silting have put the harbor about a kilometer away. Karangantu Harbor was the center of the maritime spice trade in the 16th and 17th centuries. It is the reason the first English factors were left here. Bantam's local merchants had been importing spices from the Moluccas and waiting to rip off the Europeans when they sailed in to buy them. The Dutch soon tired of price negotiations and simply torched and blockaded the town before they killed the local merchants. The English decided to join, not beat, the locals and left their factors to accumulate spices at the lower prices prevailing after the European ships sailed home.

Today, the harbor's narrow channel must be continually dredged to admit the small boats that now bring lumber from Sumatra, rather than nutmeg, pepper, cloves, and mace from farther east.

The only visible similarity to the early times is the condition of the shore itself. At low tide, it is a flat gray ooze of a beach that will suck a pair of Nikes right off your feet. It seethes with millions of burrowing crab mites and slithering mud colored slime slugs. Its airborne insects are so big they could be refuelled. It hasn't changed in four hundred years.

To those first English expats this soggy shore was their home, their office, the way in and the way out of their foreign assignment. They lived here, they debased themselves, and they died here.

And as I sat down on that oozy beach digging out my Nikes, I thought about those men and their legacy, and I could only say: "An arrack to them."

Chapter Six
The Speedboat to Battambang

During the rainy season, after a few days touring the temples of Angkor, I decided to go to the well-preserved former French capital of Northwestern Cambodia--Battambang. Battambang lies about 100 miles from Siem Reap (the closest town to Angkor). My guidebook explained I could travel by car, bus or speedboat, but speedboat was preferable because of the treacherous road conditions.

A travel agent in Siem Reap confirmed this view: "Avoid long, hot, muddy pot-holed roads," she intoned, "enjoy instead comfortable luxury of a three-hour speedboat ride across scenic Tonle Sap Lake into the Sagker River through national bird sanctuary to beautiful Battambang." I had already experienced too much of Cambodia's highways, so the speedboat option was an easy sell.

I bought a Special-For-Foreigner-Ticket and booked my luxury speedboat trip. The ticket included transport to the dock with direct hotel pick up the next morning at 6 a.m. Exactly on schedule, a mud-caked pickup truck blared its horn outside my lobby.

The pickup's bed, which was designed to, and surely had, on previous occasions, carried two cows or six pigs, was now packed with eight Western tourists plus their Everest assault size backpacks.

They sat in the rain so jammed together it looked like they would need snorkels to breathe. Luckily, by the time he collected me, even the driver recognised the capacity constraints of the truck bed and he put me and his last two victims into the cab.

At the end of the muddy rutted road, we pulled up to the boat junction, where teams of baggage porters and food sellers assaulted us. These two occupations are gender specific. Baggage porters are young men who dive over the sides of the truck bed, or in my case, through the open window of the cab, to grab your stuff and haul it all 50 feet to the pier for a dollar. Food sellers are young women who relentlessly chant: "no food on boat no food on boat no food on boat," while shoving trays of baguettes and foil triangles of "Laughing Cow" cheese at you. I can report that this treat costs twice Cambodia's average daily wage because at 6 a.m. I had not thought to bring food for the "No Food on Boat" luxury speedboat trip to Battambang.

Food bought and baggage toted, ten intrepid speedboat tourists and I crossed an oozy tidal flat on a sagging plank. We boarded a narrow wooden boat where we sat for a few minutes while the bread and cheese girls and a few Battambang hotel touts competed for our attention. The rough-hewn vessel we sat in bore no resemblance to the speedboat depicted on our "Special Price for Foreigner" tickets.

In fact, this type boat's primary function is touring foreigners around the harbor's floating village and moving bananas, tires, tin sheeting and chickens over short distances. Most of us were a little curious about this development, but one seasoned traveler explained: "This is the transport boat to take us to the speed boat moored in deeper water." About this time our crew boarded and untied us, cranked up the engine and eased us off the mud bank.

As if on cue, the seasoned traveler's prophecy of transport to a speedboat appeared true. No sooner had we reached the channel than a speedboat looking exactly like the ticket picture appeared in front of us and began chugging toward open water. It was a little strange, though, that the speedboat immediately gained 300 yards on us. It was stranger still when she accelerated past the last pier in the harbor. But when our own Cambodian Queen also passed the last pier and the crew revved her up from idle to really slow, we knew it was going to be a long day.

This vessel, which was to be our home for the rest of the day, and which we could have bought for the fares we'd paid to ride it, was a hand-made open boat about 30 feet long and 6 feet wide at the beam. The engine's ability to generate noise was inversely related to its ability to generate speed. Some of my fellow travelers had the foresight to bring earplugs. The rest of us went steadily deaf.

The boat's plywood ceiling transformed the monsoon deluges we encountered into steady dripping leaks. We sat on ancient wicker armchairs with cushions a yard dog would have scorned. Since the seats weren't fastened to the floorboards they tended to capsize when we rounded sharp bends.

Two men in their late twenties and a boy in his mid-teens crewed her. One man sat at the bow with a steering wheel. He tried to control where we went. The other man sat at the stern on top of the engine.

He tried to control how fast we got there. Both men shared the duty of hitting the engine with spanners and pipes when it conked out or whenever else they figured it needed a good bashing.

The boy had multiple responsibilities. His most important duty was lighting cigarettes for the other crewmembers. His minor duties included shouting at Engine Man to slow down to avoid swamping a pirogue or crashing into a floating tree and poling us out of the mud banks Wheel Man failed to avoid. We later discovered that Pole Boy had some vital ad hoc emergency duties, without which, this story may not have been written, or at least not written here in Battambang.

Thus appointed, we speedboat passengers entered the vast expanse of Tonle Sap Lake creeping toward distant Battambang. Tonle Sap is the largest lake in Southeast Asia. It seems like an inland sea. From the middle you can see no land in any direction. During the rainy season, its current actually flows northwest because it absorbs the overflow of the Mekong below. This was good news for us because it improved our directional speed a few knots.

Over 150 years ago, the remarkable solo explorer, Henri Mouhot, who was credited with "rediscovering" Angkor Wat, crossed Tonle Sap on a vessel probably no less seaworthy than ours. He recorded: "The entrance to the great lake of Cambodia is grand and beautiful. The river becomes wider and wider, until at last it is four or five miles in breadth; and then you enter the immense sheet of water called Tonle Sap, as large and full of motion as a sea…The waves glitter in the broad sunshine with a brilliancy which the eye can scarcely support."

Well old Henri could sugar coat a description, and maybe he was just used to being wet after two Cambodian rainy seasons, but those "glittery waves" slopped over the sides of our little launch for more than an hour. By the time we left the lake and entered the Sangker River, we were sodden and cold.

The good news about leaving the great lake and entering the river was the water was calmer and we could dry out and warm up. The bad news was that the current was now flowing against us, and as the river narrowed and became more shallow, that bad news got a lot worse. Once we entered the river, though, the sights and scenery quickly distracted us from our deliberate pace.

First, we saw fishing households. These floating accommodations, constructed of bamboo and rattan, support a bamboo hoisting contraption. The hoist is a triangle with a pulley at the apex and counterweights (usually tires or water filled plastic cans) that the fishing family use to raise an enormous net from the river whenever they think there might be fish in it. These self-contained home site/workplaces line the river for miles. We saw one lucky family pull up a net with at least 50 silvery fish flapping in it. Further upstream, we saw one emerge completely empty.

The river runs through a bird sanctuary. A pair of muscular eagles with beige and white plumage hovered low then flashed their talons into the water to snatch fish that somehow escaped the gauntlet of nets. A bird with an orange beak as long as a toucan's and bright blue feathers perched on a half-submerged tree.

Flocks of small iridescent birds changed from gold to emerald to gold as they sped past.

Housing styles changed as we moved upriver. Near the lake, water-borne houses floating on log pontoons predominated. As the river narrowed, people lived on the flat shoreline in insubstantial easy to construct bamboo sheds, as if they knew the floods would inevitably come and they would inevitably have to rebuild. Farther upstream where the riverbank was much higher, farmers built permanent wood frame houses set atop concrete pylons. Some of the conscientious homeowners here even painted their houses. Smurf Blue was the most popular color.

Agricultural occupations also evolved as we ascended the river. At the river's mouth, only fishing seemed possible because the shore was soft and inaccessible. At mid-river, farmers planted paddy fields right into the lapping edge of the water. It was already harvest time or else the rising river would have taken most of their crop. Upriver, the narrower course carved high banks where farmers planted dry-land crops like maize, sugar cane and hundreds of acres of an eight-foot-tall dark green bushy five-leafed vegetable that appeared, to my untrained eye, to be cannabis. Seeing this abundance and clearly thinking the same thing, the German sitting next to me leaned over and shouted above the engine: "It is enough for the lifetime!"

Diverse river traffic continuously passed us in both directions. Motorised long boats pulled rows of roped-up canoes piled with bamboo and wood. High-powered cargo launches carried plastic petrol containers and hardware supplies. Rough-cut pirogues paddled by a man or woman squatting at the bow moved passengers and groceries.

There was so much to see, most of us barely noticed that we hadn't been off the boat for five hours by the time Wheel Man pulled up to a petrol barge. Having drunk six cups of black Khmer coffee to neutralise the effects of a 5 a.m. wakeup; however, I was not among those who hadn't noticed. I bounded off the boat and discovered the dubious convenience of a hole cut in a rotting platform over the river at the rear of the barge.

When we powered away from the barge, Wheel Man assured me we were only two hours from Battambang. Apparently, in that calculation, he was not accounting for two engine breakdowns and a monsoon storm that would have materially raised the level of the Mississippi River.

The first engine failure coincided with the monsoon burst. We were dead stopped with Pole Boy holding us off the bank while Wheel Man and Engine Man took turns clobbering the engine with a metal pipe like they might a dog that had just stolen their lunch.

During this episode in creative mechanics the skies opened, and, frankly, metaphor fails me here, except to say that I couldn't be certain if we were on the river or under it because there was as much water above us as below us. Throughout it though, to my lasting admiration, Pole Boy held us clear of the bank.

He was as defiant as Lieutenant Dan atop "The Jenny" cursing his Creator as the hurricane wiped out the rest of Alabama's shrimp fleet in "Forrest Gump." He was as obsessed as Captain Ahab lashed to the foremast as the white whale crushed "The Pequod" in "Moby Dick." (Well, okay, maybe I was a little too close to the action to be objective), but if Pole Boy had failed, we would have had to chainsaw the boat in half to free it from the mud.

Eventually, though, as always happens in Southeast Asia, the rain suddenly stopped and for no reason that can be discerned from mechanics or nature, the engine finally responded to the beatings and cranked up.

From there, we entered a narrow twisting dangerous looking stretch of roiling brown water where the vegetation on both banks was so dense and so high it blocked the light and obstructed all views to the land beyond. I imagined the scene in "Apocalypse Now" when the Indians attack the gunboat, and the skipper gets speared, and I worried for Wheel Man.

We couldn't have been making more than two knots against the current here. Broken plants, dead animals and other debris surged past us as the engine started to struggle again. Then with a single fuel-scented puff of gray smoke, it just quit. In seconds, the current overcame our pitiful forward momentum, and we were heading backward in a hurry.

Until then, I only had a passing admiration for Pole Boy's tenacity against a raging deluge. I had seen nothing. Now, as Wheel Man rushed back to help Engine Man smash the engine into submission, Pole Boy sprang to the bow, bit down on the tow rope, and from a standing start, leapt off our moving boat across five feet of river to a slippery bank three feet above the deck. He somehow gained his footing, controlled the boat, and tied the rope to a tree. We jerked to a halt, my armchair toppled back, and I lost my last baguette to the sloshy deck.

We clung precariously to the tree for nearly an hour while wizened grannies paddling hollow logs with broom handles passed us like we were standing still. (Which thanks to the acrobatic heroics of Pole Boy, we were).

Since I am in Battambang today recording this account, you will know that the engine again cowered from its beating and restarted. The river widened and calmed. And our trusty boat limped up to the Battambang pier more than two hours later, at last completing our nine-hour "three-hour luxury speed boat ride."

When we tied up, I was amazed to see the same hotel touts we'd encountered at Siem Reap dock so long before jumping into our boat and demanding our business. "How did you get here before us?" I asked one of them. "Easy, Sir," he said. "We took the speedboat."

Chapter Seven
East Timor
Post-War Dili After Dark

[This article was written shortly after East Timor gained its independence from Indonesia in 2002 following a prolonged violent struggle]

In the solar system of Portugal's former colonial empire, East Timor was Pluto. Portugal basically abandoned it in 1975 and Indonesia annexed it the same year. In 2002, after a terrible war, East Timor (or Timor Leste) became an independent nation.

Dili, the capital of East Timor, is a tropical town noted today for fleets of "UN" stenciled Land Rovers, wall- to-wall Chubb Security installations and gaily colored coils on concertina wire. It has not quite made it to the top of the Southeast Asia holiday circuit. The surest proof of this is that no Lonely Planet Guide yet herds migratory backpackers into designated areas here.

What passes for Dili's downtown, looks, not surprisingly, like it was a war zone five years ago. Rusted car skeletons lean against the charred roofless walls of former shops, government buildings and colonial villas. Reminders of the Indonesian militias' savagery are everywhere.

But now rebuilding is somewhat underway. A few places have been built from scratch with concrete blocks, pre-form casts and more traditional materials. Other places achieved a patchwork reconstruction effect by fixing corrugated steel roofs and plastic sheeting to buildings that luckily retained four walls. However, many buildings, hopelessly damaged, still stand derelict on rubble-strewn grounds

Even beyond the effects of the war horror, though, there was probably never too much to Dili. Today, it stretches about five miles around a bay wedged between a range of scrubby red dirt hills crawling with skinny goats and the placid Flores Sea. A sand and gravel strand runs along the entire shorefront. A small central waterfront area shaded by banyans and lined with concrete benches and drinks vendors makes an early evening refuge for much of the population. But you would never call Dili a beach resort, especially if you had just de-planed from Bali.

It is a little difficult to understand why the Portuguese stayed here for so many centuries. Maybe no one cared enough to throw them out as the Dutch did in Malacca, Ceylon and the Spice Islands. Compared with other Southeast Asian capitals, even Vientiane seems frenetic. Dili's streets are wide and organized in a European style grid. Cars drive about 20 mph and the only horns blowing are from taxis soliciting business from pedestrians.

During the hot afternoons most activity stops, but things perk up a little after dark. Several of Dili's Portuguese restaurants, recently opened to rejuvenate dedicated UN workers weary from a full day of driving around town, rival Macau's.

But what about nightlife? The local tourist magazine, "Discover Dili" (the April edition of which was on sale when I visited in August) rather overstates the potential: "Nightlife in Dili offers a great variety of choices." Umm...sure. You can choose Aussie expats clobbered on VB beer, or government officials who lingered over lunch until after dark, or self-important foreign aid workers waxing ridiculous about global political trends over a nice vinho verde and grilled sea trout.

I chose the Aussies. It's easier to understand what they're talking about, their world view is more compatible with my own, and on that particular Saturday, the Tri Nations rugby match against South Africa was on TV.

In order to get a full picture of the scene, I decided to divide my time between two carefully selected spots: The Dili Club and Castaway. The Dili Club deserves special mention because it claims to have been founded in 1999. This would be about like starting up a vodka and caviar bistro during the Battle of Stalingrad. I chose Castaway because it advertised that drinking there was more stimulating than talking to volleyball named Wilson. Well, I've spent a lot of time in Aussie bars, and I'm not prepared to accept that sort of claim at face value.

I was able to do thorough research because the rugby match didn't kick off until 10 p.m. The local cuisine at both pubs was similar: chips and pizzas at Dili Club and chips and burgers at Castaway. The critical difference was Dili Club was a sports bar, whereas Castaway tripled as a bar, a dive shop, and a tattoo parlor. While the Dili Club crowd was screaming "On you Aussies," Castaway's clientele were narrating a video of undersea footage from the

Discovery Channel: "Blow me! That shark just swallowed that angler fish whole."

"Yeah, seen that once off Irian Jaya, mate!"

I left Castaway before they brought out the tattoo videos, so I never learned how many VB's it takes to drink a volleyball pretty. I returned to the Dili Club to find a mob of exuberant soldiers and a couple of curious Jesuits who got vaguely giddy when I pressed for specifics about what they did out in the bush. They all shared the agony of a South African win, and I somehow remembered the name of my hotel when I found a taxi at 2 a.m.

Not satisfied that I had done a full survey, however, I went out again on Sunday afternoon. Sunday afternoon is beach day for the multinational set in Dili. The UN boys and girls descend on Dili's only white sand beach, Areia Branca, and the neatly named Caz Bar (owned by Caz). Bamboo walls, thatched roof, beach front, cold beer, barbecued prawns and a parking lot that looks like a Land Rover showroom, pretty much sums up Caz. But at least the conversation focused on sports rather than world peace, so there must not have been many foreign aid workers about.

Outside of Caz Bar, the international helpers who preferred beach picnics to the bar scene, spread out their goodies. Unfortunately, the "Customers Only" parking lot rule meant these holidaymakers had to park against a beach wall on a road that is only about 1.1 times the width of their Land Rovers. That left plenty of room for Timorese motorbikes, but everyone else was pretty much stuck for the duration of the picnic baskets. Luckily that was well before Caz called for last orders.

I spent Monday morning at Santa Cruz cemetery, the site of the infamous massacre of Timorese civilians. It is difficult to picture what the cemetery looked like in November 1991, when Max Stahl's images alerted the outside world to East Timor's plight, because a large proportion of the graves contain the remains of Timorese who died after 1991. Worse still, an extraordinary number of infants were buried there in 1999.

I don't know how many of the remaining UN staff still focus on that grim history, but I expect their next leave and their next posting gets more conversation at the pub these days. In my view, the international military contingent needs to remain in East Timor until there is no possibility of a recurrence of the atrocities here. With Jakarta's current official attitude toward the principal suspects in these crimes, that may be a very long time. But I wonder how soon the Land Rover and beach bar crew will have finally achieved all their notable goals and the UN can send the road rally home and let East Timor get on with life.

India and Pakistan

Chapter Eight

Remembrance Of Things Pass
A Day Trip Up the Khyber

[This article was written before the attacks of
September 11, 2001]

There is a 19th Century Protestant church at the south end of Bombay's Colaba Causeway. It has a disproportionately tall steeple and before the skyline of Nariman Point was developed, it was the most prominent landmark for visitors arriving to Bombay by sea. One hundred and fifty years later, it is still a place of startling repose in that seething city. The official name of the church is St. John the Evangelist, but it has always been better known by another name – The Afgan Church. It was Imperial Britain's attempt to enshrine the memory of the soldiers and dependants who died over a 35 year period in the Anglo-Afgan Wars. Wars that now barely rate a footnote in Asia's military history.

The Church contains the usual poignant plaques in remembrance of individual officers and faded shreds of regimental colours but its essence is in a simple phrase inscribed in the chancel: "This Church built in memory of the Officers whose names are written here and of the non-commissioned Officers and Private Soldiers, too many to be so recorded, who fell, mindful of their duty by sickness or by the Sword in Afganistan."

Those Wars were fought from the 1840's to the 1870's to give British India what the Germans would later call "Lebensraum." They were fought hand to hand against the mountain tribesmen to shut down the easiest access of Russians, Persians, Turks, Uzbeks into India – the Kyber Pass. In 1947, after all the bother, Britain bequeathed the Pass to nascent Pakistan.

Today, after the recent years of Afgans fighting Russians and each other and streams of refugees crossing east to Pakistan, it is again fairly easy for a Western tourist with some resources to visit the Khyber Pass to try to imagine what on Earth those Brits were thinking way back then. All that is really required today is to find yourself in Peshawar with more money than brains and a free morning on your hands.

After three days in Peshawar, it was not too difficult for me to meet those simple tests. I'd done all the bazaars, where I'd been offered hashish by about one-half of the adult population. I'd been to the main mosque at mid-day on a Friday. I'd been up the Swat Valley to the Silk Road. I couldn't get a tee time at the golf club until three o'clock. So off I went.

As with anything in South Asia, logistics is key. The first order of business is to find one of those multi-tasking driver/guide/fixers that the subcontinent is so full of. Mine, Zulfaqar, took me to the Khyber Agency permit post at the Army Cantonment where I got the permit for a few rupees, but more importantly, where we picked up Masbooq, the Assassin, a black clad soldier with a Kalashnikov and a bag of cartridge clips who we deposited in the back seat as an equalizer to the Afridi tribesmen who like to set up informal toll stations in their neighbourhoods. We drove west out of Peshawar through a rambling free form market called Smugglers Bazaar to a barrier that said "No foreigners beyond this point". What it really meant was no foreigners without a Masbooq in the backseat.

Past that sign, the driver explained, the Peshawar police exercise no authority and it did seem like everything was available. The main street was a weapons emporium. I saw grenade launchers, mortars, every kind of automatic and semi-automatic weapon. You could probably get anti-aircraft guns and missiles if you had the patience. Less obvious but surely there according to Zulfaqar was a pharmacopea of narcotics as well as Muslim banned substances like Heineken.

After 3 or 4 kilometers of this laisser faire enterprise, we reached a check point where Zulfaqar actually did have to produce documentary evidence that I'd given my rupees to the Army post. Remarkably a European was trying to achieve the same passage by himself with no Zulfaqar or Masbooq and with the predictable result that he was still at the same place hours later when we returned from the Afgan border.

Past the check point there is an archway and small monument to all of the various people who had stopped by over the last 4000 years, a "George Washington slept here" for Eastern Civilization. Beginning with the Vedic-era Aryans, to Alexander the Great, to the Arabs, to Babur the first Mogul Emperor, to the British, and now the Afganis themselves fleeing first the Russians and now the Taliban, they all came through the Pass.

The road ascends from the archway over a landscape that could be fairly described as rubble and through an atmosphere of suspended dust baked in a 45°C haze. There are occasional adobe style villages set in small palm oases surrounded by high walls. There are ruined Buddhist stupas from the Gandhara civilization that have stood for two millennia. There is a new fortified palace 800 meters on a side with electronic surveillance and patrolling guards which Zulfaqar helpfully explained belonged to a local "businessman."

Throughout the pass, the British had somehow built guard posts high on the mountain tops to snipe at intruders. The narrowest point in the pass, originally about five meters wide, called Ali Masjid, was heavily protected and marked with a sign commemorating Alexander the Great's visit.

The first paved road through the Pass was built by the British Army during the Great Game era. It still roughly exists below the post independence tarmac which we took. Traditional type smugglers prefer the old road with donkey and camel caravans of goodies for the Pakistan border bazaars. The new road is the province of the 20th century truck trade in TV's, CD players and weapons. But the most amazing economic traffic through the Pass is in bicycle transport. The bicycle entrepreneurs catch a truck across the Afgan border some 50 km and 500 meters in elevation away from Peshawar's bazaars and ride back on one bike with two more strapped to the sides. I never saw them dismount even on the steepest grades. Their profit margin for the trip was 50 rupees. I'll never understand why Pakistan doesn't enter a team in Le Tour sponsored by some local munitions firm.

In addition to road building, the natural landscape was also altered by the construction of the Khyber Railway during the early twentieth century. The tracks of the Khyber Railway weave between and over the old and new roads. This railway was a stupendous feat of imperial British engineering. The effort to build it, with its dozens of bridges and tunnels, switch backs and block houses, is reminiscent of the construction of the city of New Delhi or perhaps even the Suez Canal. It is a monument to what an absolute ruler can achieve with unlimited resources and free labour.

The original idea of the Railway was to be able to move troops quickly to the border to stop advancing Whoevers from penetrating the exposed northwestern flank of British India. In fact, it may have done as much duty as a quick get away from the same Whoevers if the results of the first couple of Anglo-Afgan Wars are any measure. Today, a train still occasionally runs to the village of Landi Kotal, halfway to the border, for touring railway buffs. But there the tracks stop and the remainder of the line is in a state of abandoned disrepair with collapsed trellises and caved-in tunnels. It is the Ozymandiaz of imperial civil engineering.

Landi Kotal itself is worth one trip. It is a small trading town on a desolate mesa where donkey herders transfer title to pick-up drivers and disappear back into the mountains. Business here is conducted at the primordial level. You put down your stuff, you pick up the money, and you back away with your hand on your gun. People move around in small groups. Even the soldiers cluster together. The air is opaque and sickening from the exhaust of rows of idling trucks.

It might have been oxygen deprivation, but in the middle of all this, I strangely recalled a scene from the first Star Wars movie. It was that bleak, threatening gallactic outpost, Mos Eisley, where Luke Skywalker first met Han Solo and chartered the Millenium Falcon. The transport available in Landi Kotal is a little slower and there are a lot more Wookies. But there are eerie similarities in the landscape, and in the chaotic intensity, and in the irrespressible desire of an outsider to make a quick exit.

Beyond Landi Kotal are only more check points and more donkeys until you reach the end of the tour at a vista near the border town of Torkhan, as far as a foreign tourist can travel even with Masbooq. If you peer out from there through the haze onto the arid plains of Taliban Afganistan and reflect back on your short passage and the long history, the potential for melee becomes suddenly palpable.

The Pass has always been a battle ground simply because it is navigable; because it is the way in and the way out of the subcontinent. It is the escape route the British army was seeking in 1842 when they retreated from Kabul and were slaughtered at Gandamack. It is the place they fought the Pathans to a bloody standoff thirty years later when modern warfare technology first met its match in determined Islamic resistance, and, as Kipling noted, "two thousand pounds of education drops to a ten rupee jezail." It is the place Russian tanks and gunships could not subdue the Mujahadeen and where now U.S. Tomahawk missiles only temporarily shatter the camps of those early tribesmen's descendants, who will return just as they always have.

Even today on the Pakistan side, almost everyone in the Pass appears to be armed. The soldiers, the smugglers, the tea sellers, the cyclists, the camel drivers, strap automatic rifles on their backs. They shout at each other and argue over small slights. They look at you furtively, indirectly, and as the only Westerner around, you quickly comprehend the futility of fighting these people. And you remember that old Protestant church at the edge of Bombay and its sad inscription. And you remember the non-commissioned Officers and Private Soldiers, too many …

Chapter Nine
Bombay Beach Party
The Ganesh Festival
[Bombay is now called Mumbai]

In India's Vedic pre-history, the son of Shiva and Parvati began his journey toward immortality when his father mistakenly lopped off his head with a sword, and upon realizing his mistake, replaced his son's head with one of a passing elephant. That son goes by the names of Ganesh and Ganapati. He is commonly depicted throughout India as chubby, smiling and a little mischievous.

Ganesh's devotees ascribe to him the ability to grant wisdom and wealth. This makes him probably the most popular deity in the Hindu pantheon. To repay Ganesh's bounty in Bombay, every year around September, in the Hindu month of Bhadra, virtually the entire Hindu population of the city celebrates his birth in the ten-day festival of Ganesh Chaturthi.

During the Ganesh festival, devotees purchase small images for their homes, and professional craftsmen mold enormous clay images, which are set up in pavilions throughout the city. On the tenth day of the holiday, or "puja," all the industrial-sized clay images are loaded on flatbed trucks. The smaller ones travel in the back seat of cars or are simply carried by hand on the urban railways to the beaches of the city. There, this most beneficent of gods is subjected to the annual indignity of being immersed and dissolved in the fetid waters of the Arabian Sea.

The festival actually has secular origins. It began as a way for the Indian independence movement to circumvent the British ban on public assembly during the late 19th century. But whatever its origins, the event is now a colossal celebration, and perhaps the world's largest religion-inspired beach party.

Processions from all over Bombay commandeer the city's already congested road system, riding upon or walking beside the doomed Ganapatis. Loudspeakers shriek from the truck cabs and marchers bang drums and gongs, while orange-capped devotees on the back of the trucks shower themselves and everyone in their wake with red powder called "gulal."

The most popular destination for these processions is Chowpatty Beach. It is a curved strip of sand about a kilometer long at the north end of posh Marine Drive.

On normal days, Chowpatty serves as the city's permanent carnival site, homeless shelter and pony riding school. On puja day, though, it is ablaze with high intensity lighting and crowded with more trucks than a major highway depot. The decibel level from the competing speakers would register between deafening and fatal. Amidst it all, thousands of families spread blankets and consume picnics.

They come to see the infinite variety of shapes, postures and personalities the Ganesh makers have brought to their art during their months of preparation. Dozens of the normal pink ones sitting in a yogic pose are brought, as well as standing ones with a benevolent hand lifted. But there are also many more worldly ones with flashing lights or festooned with coins.

My favorite was a gigantic yellow god playing a sitar sitting on a blue globe. Whatever the style of their Ganesh, however, all worshipers share one experience when they arrive at the beach. After they have lavished him with garlands and powder and presented him, according to their own preferences, with offerings of fruit and flowers. After they have performed, according to their own faith, their private devotions to him. They must all face one final unifying question: "How in the world are we going to get this ten-foot tall, 500-kilogram statue off the back of this truck and down to the sea without a forklift?"

Well, don't ask me, but somehow, they all do it. Most of them seemed to be loosely organized into truck bed crews and beach assault divisions. The guys on the truck shove and muscle the image off the back. Then the landing force, stripped to loin cloths, take it onto their shoulders and, with knees buckling like an over-ambitious weightlifter failing to finish a snatch, they stumble headlong, like a drunken centipede toward the surf screeching, "Ganapati Bappa Morya, Ganapati Bappa Morya,"

I don't know any Indian languages, but from the reaction of the bystanders, I believe this chant roughly translates: "Half-ton statue coming through. Move your butt or lose it—NOW!!!"

When they reach the sea, with or without a couple of bodies underfoot, they carry the elephant god into the water and attempt to turn him flat and push out to sink and dissolve. Some don't succeed. A poignant sight is a few of the especially buoyant and bottom-heavy ones sitting upright and floating several hundred meters from shore as if they had begun a long journey to East Africa. I hope they made it.

The party continues until after midnight when the last Ganesh is launched, and the beach is finally returned to its indigenous homeless sleepers and fishing families. In the morning, it resembles an Indian version of New Orleans on Ash Wednesday, with flotsam of marigolds quietly washing ashore alongside undissolved elephant trunks and palm frond garlands.

The clean-up crews and scavengers go to work early, and, by afternoon, the beach is back to its normal state of clutter to lie dormant for another year, while the Makers of the Gods replenish their storehouses and wait for the frenzy to renew.

Chapter Ten
Leopold Café Bombay

[This article was written before the 2008 terrorist attack on the Leopold, and around the time Gregory David Roberts, author of "Shantaram," was a frequent visitor. The menu and drinks selection have dramatically improved since, but the upstairs disco is gone]

To view the latest fashion in body piercing, tattooing, head shaving and East/West cross dressing there are few better galleries than the Leopold Cafe & Bar on Colaba Causeway in Bombay. The Brits founded it in 1871 as a chemist's shop. One hundred years ago a Parsee family took over and converted it into a restaurant.

Today the Leopold is an intersection on the Asian backpacking route. It is also an essential refuge, an oasis of comparative repose in one of Asia's most frenetic cities. Bombay can bite you. I have seen seasoned independent travelers crying for their mothers and sophisticated foreign businessmen crying for their pensions. And I have joined them. But an hour in the Leopold will always bring me back to the serene state of lunacy that helps me endure that Great City.

Besides the backpackers, the Leopold fills up with East Africans, Arabs on beer breaks, Bombay yuppies in designer gear and middle-aged Western tourists who either bought the Lonely Planet guide or just got lost. Many patrons sit for hours reading their guidebooks and novels and scratching in their diaries. Younger travelers swap intelligence on cheap hotels, bhang lassi and nipple rings, while the older salaried-types like me tend to sit near the back to plan or recover from another business day.

The building itself is well matured. The nicotine patina of the yellow walls, dingy mirrors and anything else that has been there more than two weeks is on form. The de rigueur "languid overhead fans" could do service in a Somerset Maugham or Joseph Conrad novel. My favourite feature is the oversize doorway that opens onto the manic street. It's a sanitary observation deck to "real Bombay" with its hawkers, moneychangers, urchins, and beggars of every affliction, all kept safely at bay by lathi-wielding guards.

The Leopold occupies two stories of a corner building. Each storey has its own character although neither would qualify as a proper Western-style bar. Downstairs is open air with seating in wooden chairs around tightly packed square tables. Three plastered columns with gold scrolled capitols hold up the ceiling and obscure the views of the chaos outside and the fashion show inside.

The walls are decorated with posters of Bogart, Elvis and James Dean. The Parsee Eagle-Man icon is prominent throughout. A long mural of quirky cartoons of "Life at the Leopard" is painted along the far wall above the service counter. The counter itself is ladened with pyramids of bright tropical fruit stacked on rows of beer cans. Sadly, the fruit is not available for daiquiris because the drinks list downstairs is simply: "Draft Beer, Beer (Canned), Beer (Small Bottles), Beer (Large Bottles)".

Seat selection downstairs is crucial. The power centre is to the left of the middle column. It is ideal for viewing and for access to waiters who must walk past you whether they want to or not. If you sit too close to the open doorways, your chances of participating in the street show, rather than just watching it, increase dramatically. Beggars' upturned palms often thrust into the premises. They can quickly turn into down-turned fists taking your chapattis south down the Causeway if you look away. At a minimum, you will need to deal with the droning chorus for alms directed personally at you rather than generally at greater society.

It can all tend to put you off your food, which would be a shame because the food is not that bad. The quantities are ample, and in over thirty trips to the Leopold, I cannot remember having thrown up a meal. I can vaguely recall an occasion when I chundered an overdose of local rum consumed during a sectarian riot lockdown, but I am virtually certain I have never blown lunch. This is a startling record for any Indian eatery.

There is a regular and a Chinese menu. Chinese food includes the intriguing specialities of "Wanton Soup" (sic) and "Wanton Noodles". The rest of the menu is less provocative and more predictable. They serve curries, every kind of egg dish, chicken, fish and chips, and anything with rice. But the main culinary event is the fantastic enormous, fresh, soft, piping hot naan. These naan are the size and shape of a Salvador Dali depiction of a deflated rugby ball.

The naan have the scientifically verified capacity to soak up the alcohol of three large Kingfisher beers with the unfortunate side effect of leaving very little room for more large Kingfishers! This situation often provokes the late-night imbiber, fired up on Wanton Soup, to venture upstairs to the Leopold disco and SWITCH TO RUM!!! (See previous warning about pursuing this strategy during sectarian riot lockdowns).

Upstairs is completely different. It is a loud, dark, savagely air-conditioned disco, but luckily you can't hear it or see it from below. I would still be ignorant of its virtues if I hadn't been sharing a downstairs table with a young English guy who had attracted the attention of a young English girl with a newly installed nose stud. When she came to our table and asked him to follow her upstairs, he looked at me and said, "I just got engaged, mate, would you mind doing the chaperone bit?" So up we went. Unlike downstairs, there is a doorkeeper to the disco. It is not clear exactly what admission criteria he applies, but occasionally people do get turned back. If you pass inspection (as you will with an English girl beside you) you go through the blackened glass door into Leopold's parallel universe.

Flashing lights and pounding speakers surround a small illuminated dance floor. A bar in the corner dispenses oceans of rum and other local spirits much of which ends up on the floor. Clusters of Indians guys in open shirts and gold chains smoke cigarettes and troll for white chicks. It has a quaint charm---a certain South Asian "je ne sais quois".

It takes new visitors from downstairs a little time or a few rums to adjust to this environment. Foreigners will feel more alien. Despite this, I can't remember ever having a really bad time there. And once I've taken the dubious decision to go up, I usually stay until closing. I am unfortunately not able to report precisely when the disco closes because I have never been quite capable of telling time when I left. Closing hours do, however, appear to have something to do with the last man out, which has a lot to do with the last white chick out.

I once took a research assistant upstairs to help me remember what it was like and what time it closed. She left with an Indian guy in an open shirt and gold chains before she finished her research. Although I haven't seen her since, I imagine her recollection of the experience would differ from mine.

But never mind when you leave, or whether, until then, you sensibly sat downstairs sipping beer and scribbling post cards, or wantonly went upstairs and lost your way. The important point is that the Leopold opens early every day, even during sectarian riots.

Chapter Eleven
Calcutta Images
[Calcutta is now called Kolkota]

Beggars drone for alms. Rickshaw pullers ring warning bells. Shop owners hawk for custom. Honking taxi drivers shout solicitations at passing foreigners. And everywhere, there are people, people, people. If Calcutta's streetside cacophony begins to overwhelm you, lift your gaze from the human crush of her dusty pavements to contemplate the grandeur of her oldest buildings.

Calcutta's decomposing colonial architectural elegance whispers the splendour of the British Empire above the chaos, congestion and sometime squalor of today's seething city. Unlike other former imperial capitals, where glass and steel replaced the Georgian and Neo-Classical monuments to power and money, much of Calcutta's colonial architectural heritage, in varying states of disrepair, remains.

The domed earth-bound Victoria Memorial, fronted by a supremely unamused visage of the Queen-Empress herself, stands in view of the glistening white spire of St. Paul's Cathedral.

Nearby, on Calcutta's green-lung Maidan, smoky fires warm homeless people and whatever eatable things they have managed to scavenge. Scattered cricket matches entertain anyone who has time to play or watch.

Down a well-groomed gravel drive, behind wrought iron gates and guardhouses, elected politicians now occupy the British Viceroys' baronial palace. Indian civil servants now toil in the cavernous red brick Writers' Building where expatriate clerks of the East India Company once tallied opium profits.

Wigged and robed Indian barristers and judges administer an English-modeled system of justice in the gothic Law Courts where the Crown's Writ ran for more than two hundred years.

Hindustani trading firms now occupy the ornate British banking and insurance headquarters that preside over the city's traffic-choked intersections.

Even though victim to neglect, pollution, overcrowding and swampy climate, Calcutta's buildings still transmit an arrogant voice from a distant age that says: "Here we rule. Look upon our works."

Today, you look upon their works as if they were the fossilized evidence of some extinct predator and you ask: "Why did they become so huge, then die out so suddenly?"

Or you look upon them as if they were the ruins of what some ancient civilization abandoned to the jungles of Cambodia or the Yucatan and you ask: "Why did they build such beauty in this fetid place, then leave it all behind?"

Before you begin to consider these mysteries, follow the timeless example of Calcutta's late colonial masters by taking refuge from the heat and grime in a shady hotel garden surrounded by a full supply of gin and tonic. The answers will soon be obvious.

Chapter Twelve
This Other Eden

The Great Calcutta Cricket Riot

After many years living in Hong Kong, I had begun to believe I had completed the difficult transition from a baseball to a cricket fan. I was no longer surprised when an otherwise rational person puts his face inches from the path of a ball that can come off a bat in excess of 100 miles per hour. I was no longer confused by the endless commentary about the state of the wicket--whether it is holding up or taking turn. And most encouragingly, I was no longer tongue-tied by names like Arjuna Ranatunga, Sachin Tendulkar, and Wasim Akram. The only thing left was to attend a world-class match.

I decided to start at the top with a pilgrimage to the high temple of Asian Cricket--Eden Gardens, Calcutta for a World Cup semi-final between Sri Lanka and India. Calcutta as a city and a match venue is a full-frontal assault. It is the entire experience.

Another American and I entered this parallel universe through Dum Dum airport around midnight the night before the match. We were met by Driver Ali. He had miraculously elbowed his way through an angry crowd of taxi touts to rescue us. We climbed into his ancient Ambassador car and bounced off into the Bengali night toward our guesthouse. After some confusion about the difference between address number 3 and 3A (A missing), we were eventually admitted to our accommodation by Mahavinda, the housekeeper. Mahavinda was a personable but uncommunicative chap, who through various grunts and sign language was able to show us to a room and produce tea at predictable intervals when he was not sleeping on the living room floor in the only *dhoti* he has ever owned.

The morning of the match, after a failed attempt to motivate Mahavinda to fix breakfast, our tickets arrived. It was an afternoon start, so with time on our hands, we took off with Driver Ali for some sightseeing at the old Howrah Bridge. The bridge spans the River Hooghli from North Calcutta to Howrah ("City of Joy") and it is an instructive microcosm for Calcutta and its cricket.

The bridge itself was so burdened with human and vehicular traffic that it swayed and creaked like a full stadium. Across it, bearers ladened with cargo ran back and forth in the kind of desperation the chasing side shows when the target is too high. Beside it, the older ones, in their final overs, sat in hopeless defiance of their certain fate. And everywhere, the privileged and impoverished for a short time conjoined on this single path in a bedlam of noise and smoke.

Metaphorically, we needn't have gone farther, but we'd paid for the tickets, so we found Ali and headed back. Ali drove through the seething inner city on streets choked down with rickshaws and pushcarts, buses, trucks, trams and cars. When the streets became impossibly jammed, he ducked down alleys lined with naked children glistening from their gutter-side baths. Wherever he turned were fumes and exhaust and horns and horns and horns.

The melee reminded me of that moment of revelation in the movie, "City of Joy," when the rickshaw tycoon, told Patrick Swayze that the rich in Calcutta erect a Wall out of money to separate "us" from "them". Well, this "us" knew which side of that Wall we belonged on--the side serving beers and lunch next to swimming pools, and that is exactly what we found at the Oberoi Grand Hotel.

After a couple of refreshing hours, it was time to walk to the stadium. Fortified, but still innocent, we went back into the streets to join a crowd shuffling towards the grounds in a herding instinct reminiscent of migrating wildebeests oblivious to lions. Our herd shoved through the broken tarmac lanes reserved for the few predatory vehicles approaching Eden. As humans and machines converged, my New York City instinct to show no fear and keep walking, soon gave way to the practical view that when a car actually nudges you, a little fear is no disgrace.

When we finally reached the gates separating people from autos, I was surprised to see the police confiscating newspapers from fans. After all, cricket can be a bit slow at times, and there is a long interval between innings.

Our seats were on the High Court End separated from the rabble by barbed wire fences. Our immediate neighbours were elite northern Indians and rich Bangladeshis with U.S. cash.

Everyone knew the game so well their discourse sounded like familiar poetry recited. A teenage

Bangladeshi girl next to us who backed Sri Lanka could tell the names of every player on the pitch. A row of privileged Indian kids behind us with faces painted in orange, white and green, chanted full voiced in what a Calcutta newspaper later deplored as broken Hindi in the Pakistani style.

On the pitch India won the toss and put Sri Lanka in to bat first. After a shaky start losing two wickets in the first over, Sri Lanka managed to put up a decent but reachable score of 251 to the jubilation of the home crowd.

At the interval, we left the stadium for snacks and beers at the venerable but decidedly dirty, and now sadly demised, Great Eastern Hotel. The only setbacks there were the live bugs in the bottom of our beer glasses and the unexplained black specks on our cheese sandwiches. Shored up, but with new health concerns, we returned to Eden for what everyone expected would be a comfortable Indian progression to the final. Events diverged.

A good opening from Tendulkar, which left our young Bangladeshi fan discouraged, was followed in quick succession by a staccato fall of wickets. After the loss of four the painted kids fell silent. Minutes later wickets 5 and 6 fell as restlessness succeeded despair throughout the High Court End. When number 7 was out with India still 130 runs adrift, the mood was as ominous as the warm yellow wind that whips through the American Plains in advance of tornadoes. Then suddenly, as if fulfilling the preordained denouement of an enormous tragedy, the new batsman gently lifted his first ball for an easy out to turn a simple loss into an historic butt-kicking and the crowd took command of Eden.

Hundreds of water bottles were lofted onto the pitch. In seconds, we understood the police interest in newspapers. Eden fans prize them not for accurate reporting or insightful commentary but for combustion. They burn fast, and on a breezy night they burn hot enough to ignite the cardboard posters Coca Cola so thoughtfully handed out.

In the cheap seats of the High Court End the fans organized themselves into tactical units. The strong arms bombarded the pitch with bottles and the ones with matches lit everything except their own clothes. But at top of the destruction hierarchy, was the ballistics group, who had managed to smuggle "crackers" into the stands. These crackers are as similar to the things Americans pop off on Independence Day as sparklers are to hand grenades. They are industrial explosives so loud they would make a dead man jump. And to our misfortune, the tier right behind us had most of them.

This episode of constructive fan criticism lasted about half an hour while the players huddled in the dressing rooms and the unarmed foreign spectators ducked for cover. After most of the people who hadn't brought weapons had left the stadium and the police had begun to roam the stands with *lathis*, things quietened. Then, to my undying amazement, the teams were sent back onto the field with the apparent expectation of bringing this sporting debacle to the anti-climax of pathetic India losing her last two wickets.

Well, the High Court End was not having it. They were through watching cricket. They rained ammunition onto the grounds until the umpires called off the match. When the bottles were finally exhausted, and the crackers went silent we picked our way through the rubble back to the Grand Hotel for recuperative gin and tonics.

The epilogue came the next morning when our grunting friend handed us tea and the newspapers, which condemned the violence and predicted it would taint the world's image of Calcutta…not likely.

Island Nations

Chapter Thirteen
Up A Mangrove Channel In Micronesia
Kayaking In Kosrae

"Whenever you come to a fork in the channel go left," the owner of my hotel said as he prepared a kayak for me to paddle into the Mutunnenea Channel in northeastern Kosrae, Micronesia. "Eventually you'll come to a tight place where you'll have to turn back. Try not to get stuck and please watch the time. After dark you will get hopelessly lost," he warned as he launched me onto the sludgy swamp.

Kosrae is the smallest and easternmost state in the Federated States of Micronesia. It lies more than 2000 miles southwest of Hawaii and is home to about 7000 friendly, religious, self-sufficient people. Mangrove forests surround mountainous Kosrae Island. The Mutunnenea Channel carves paths through a couple of miles of those forests near the basalt ruins of the ancient royal capital, Lelu.

Kosrae legend holds that a giant snake carved the meandering channel while searching for his daughter, who had been abducted by the King of Lelu.

Inexplicably, the daughter was human, or at least looked human enough to attract the king's attention. When the snake reached Lelu, the king trapped it in a palace building. Then he set a fire that killed the snake and also, predictably, the daughter who jumped into the flames in despair.

The first thing I noticed about the Mutunnenea channel is that snorkeling is not an option. The water is the color and consistency of agitated Turkish coffee. Only at its shallowest edges is anything visible below the water surface. But my attention quickly switched from swamp water to luxuriant forest foliage when I emerged from the sheltered launch area.

Near the ocean, where I entered, the channel is as wide as a river. The outgoing tide offered some resistance to my upstream efforts, but paddling was easy enough and the view was splendid. In the tropical sun, the foliage of the main channel shines luminous gold-green like a parrot racing above a rain forest canopy. But when the sun descends behind the profile of Kosrae's Sleeping Lady Mountain or is obscured by the dark clouds that often clutter the late afternoon sky, the color subdues to the gray-blue of a heron lurking in shade.

After a quarter hour paddling, I reached my first directional decision. Two mangrove islands divided the channel into three courses—wide to the left, narrow in the middle, and "You must be joking!" to the right. Ignoring local advice, I chose the right-hand, reef-side course and was soon rewarded with the chance to practice kayak reversal at an impassable fallen tree.

Brown bubbles of muddy foam previously churned up by my paddle provided a useful navigational aid back to open water. I chose the recommended left-hand channel when I re-emerged. As I paddled on, the Mutunnenea continued offer me new "Y" intersection choices. Chastened by my first misstep, I took all turns to the left into the denser forest, away from the reef, as the waterway dramatically narrowed and darkened with each turn.

The tightest passages, where the forest tries to crowd out its own watery life, mysteriously attract kayakers. They draw you in, even though you know you may be grounded in the brown ooze or wedged into a clutch of roots. The more narrow and twisting and shallow the water path, the greater attraction to enter, and the greater the reward. Forest plants up here differ from those in the open spaces of the ocean end of the channel.

Back in the wide sunny sections, where the water is saltier, plant foliage descends to the waterline. But in the narrow interior fresh water influenced passages, the lower trunks, branches and aerial roots of the trees, standing permanently in shadow, bear few leaves. Instead, they are adorned with thick furry mosses as rich and verdant as an English summer pasture and with long streamers of fern fronds cascading like a pyrotechnic display.

Kosraens have given names to their mangrove plants: Sakasric, Flo Fol, Shrael, Fals, Melukluk, Tui. They find them useful for firewood, carving, roof thatching, furniture making and traditional medicines, as well as for trapping tourists' kayaks.

Science primers explain that the trees and other plants of mangrove forests thrive in intertidal sheltered tropical areas. These plants survive where other species cannot because they have salt filtering aerial roots and salt excreting leaves.

The oxygen breathing, salt extracting roots are obvious. They come in two types: Prop Roots of the Sakrasric look like buttresses propping up the plant's main trunk. Pneumataphores of the Flo Foi and Shrael spike up sharply from the swamp floor like aquatic stalagmites to snorkel air during low tide. Besides those species, Fals is a trunkless palm. Melukluk is a broad-leafed fern growing high in the branches of host trees. The dense stands of the Tui congest the low shoreline with ribbony networks tight-bunched over-lapping roots.

These forests buffer the mainland against storm and wave damage, and they absorb and recycle sediment runoff. (This latter function accounts for the Turkish coffee consistency of the water).

Science books do not, however, mention the inner forests' mystique and the spirits they possibly harbor. A botanically challenged tourist, like myself, paddling into the upper regions of the Mutunnenea may not be able to identify the diverse species he encounters. But if he is alert, he may imagine creatures petrified in the dense forest; and he may wonder about the snake story.

At first, he might see a majestic moose head with furry green antlers, or a dragon's neck arching toward him with its gapping mouth, or a wooden lemur hanging upside-down, reaching into the water for fruit. But later, in the dappled shadows, after he passes under a branch so low that he must lie back flat in his kayak to clear, he will notice the eyes. They aren't really eyes, are they? They are probably something like knot holes, but they appear to grant sight to forest shapes of a watching dog, serpent, boar, ram, rhinoceros.

If the eyes don't deter him, he reaches a curtain of aerial roots as dense as the beaded entrance to an Oriental parlor. The curtain appears impenetrable, but with effort he can push the thin rigid roots aside as they grab for his paddle.

Beyond this curtain, he quietly floats beneath rows of long thick pods, each suspended above his head by a single vine. In this jungle setting, he might recall the bodies hanging above the riverine entrance to Colonel Kurtz's Cambodian lair in "Apocalypse Now."

Here the brush scrapes his face and his boat; the light dims; and he struggles to paddle through root spikes emerging from the receding swamp. Here the forest not only sees; it speaks. Circles of mouths hollowed through twisted un-green trunks silently howl: "Turn back, Intruder. This place is forbidden."

Suddenly a sleek white "Sik" bird, with its long twin tail, bursts out of the gloom and jets low overhead like a vapor trail, shrieking: "No No No No." And that was enough weirdness for me. I retreated as quickly as my arms and the swamp's obstructions would allow, and it was not too soon.

I had thought the impending darkness was caused by the shadowy forest cover, but when I reached a wider passage and could see the sky again, I realized there was another, more serious reason. The sun was setting. Then I remembered something my host had warned about an ominous connection between darkness and hopelessness.

My leisurely sightseeing float was now a K-1 sprint final. With the tide at my back, I barely reached my hotel before anyone needed to interrupt cocktail hour to search for me.

I pulled my kayak onto the landing and stumbled, muddy and wet, into the hotel bar. I wanted to announce to the gathered drinkers that a giant snake had surely carved Mutunnenea and that malevolent spirits haunted its upper reaches. But a waitress distracted me with the offer of cold beer. And the moment was lost.

Chapter Fourteen

On the Soggy Trail of Somerset Maugham
In American Samoa

A thick drizzle soaked me one Saturday afternoon in Pago Pago, American Samoa. [Pronounced something like: Pango Pango]. But the drizzle was a welcome relief from the Deluge of Heaven that had just raced across the harbor driving even the most hardened denizens of the Yacht Club from their beachfront perches to the shelter of the bar.

I waited with them for the rain to slacken, but when Happy Hour ended and the price of Vailima Samoa Beer surged, I went out to find a one of the pickup truck/taxis that ply the road to town.

My truck only went as far as the main market. I was still about a mile from my hotel. But at least I was able to secure a sack of cheaper Vailimas to store against Sunday. Sunday, most drinks sellers in Pago, deferring to generations of missionaries' efforts, shut down.

Between the market and my hotel, I splashed past a colonial-style building called Sadie Thompson's Inn. I don't know whether it was the horrific weather, or the obvious pervasiveness of the missionaries' presence here; or whether I was just missing the seamier side of Honolulu, but I suddenly recalled story of the missionary-prostitute conflict Somerset Maugham told in "Rain."

"Rain" was set in Pago Pago and recounted the moral struggle between an American missionary, Rev. Davidson, and a Hawaii prostitute named Sadie Thompson. Maugham wrote "Rain" after a measles quarantine detained him and fellow steamship passengers for two weeks in Pago Pago.

Sadie Thompson's Inn is supposedly the site of the boarding house where Maugham and other stranded passengers, including Rev. Davidson, his wife and Sadie sheltered. Maugham and other reluctant and miserable boarders cowered against a rain "that rattled on the roof of corrugated iron with a steady persistence that was maddening, that seemed to have a fury of its own."

But Sadie, undeterred, set up shop. Sailors, gramophone music, dancing, liquor, right under the horrified noses of Pago Pago's polite but sodden society. The missionary, with time on his hands, and sensing a God-sent chance to dispense divine justice, took on the cause of Sadie. At first, she was outgunned. The missionary convinced the colony's American governor to deport her to San Francisco to face a prison term arising from her prior indiscretions there.

But just as life was looking darkest for a suddenly surprisingly repentant Sadie; with the 'Frisco bound steamer's departure imminent; the missionary scored an own goal in the eternal game of Good against Evil by sleeping with Sadie. Maugham quickly tidied up the loose ends of the plot with the missionary's suicide and Sadie's reprieve.

The Reverend's body was scarcely cold when she cranked up the gramophone, summoned the sailors and pronounced the benediction: "You men! You filthy dirty pigs! You're all the same, all of you. Pigs! Pigs!"

Whether the missionary versus hooker story is fact or myth is still debated in this town that has little else of historical consequence to debate. I variously heard that Sadie went on to establish a brothel. Or she took in laundry by day and turned solo tricks by night. Or local police loaded her unconscious onto a Sydney-bound steamer. Or she fell into a taboo love affair with a Samoan noble and had to return to Honolulu.

You pick. But I think Somerset would be surprised that his representative of a victory of vice over salvation became the namesake of one of this devoutly Christian community's finest restaurants. And poetically, one of the only bars that is open on Sunday.

Sadie's Inn is a culinary oasis in this land of eggs, hamburgers, Spam, pancakes and Bud Lite served in Styrofoam cups of crushed ice. One day Maugham complained that at the old boarding house they were "eating hamburger steaks again. It seems to be the only dish the cook knew how to make." Well, you can still eat hamburger steak at Sadie's, if you prefer it to salmon sushi or imported lobster, but now you can wash your burger down with a fine New Zealand Pinot Noir.

A few things have changed since Maugham's visit. From the Inn's veranda you no longer look across the harbor at sailing schooners, steamships and navy rowing launches, but at container ships and luxury cruise liners. (The Queen Mary was there during my visit). On the far shore, the coconut plantations and taro patches Somerset or Sadie might have seen through the mist and rain have yielded to the massive tuna canning plants of StarKist and Chicken of the Sea.

Many more things, however, remain remarkably the same. Sadie's indictment of Pago Pago as a "one horse burg" may seem a little harsh today. But the two-lane tarmac running between the edge of the ancient caldera that forms Pago's harbor and the impenetrable wall of jungle that juts vertically from the back of the shore is essentially the "American-built high road' that Maugham described.

On shopping, he reported that the "natives came to barter pineapples and huge bunches of bananas, tapa cloth, necklaces of shells or sharks teeth, kava bowls and model boats." If you add T-shirts and post cards to that list and put those barterers' progeny into shop houses instead of quayside canoes, the scene would be current.

His descriptions of the heat and the rain are timeless: "On land the heat, though early in the morning is already oppressive. Closed in by the hills, not a breath of air came into Pago Pago. The rain was unmerciful and somehow terrible. You felt the primitive powers of nature. And sometimes you felt that you must scream if it did not stop, and then suddenly you felt powerless, as though your bones had suddenly become soft, and you were miserable and hopeless."

Writing this, I sit, miserable and hopeless, on Sadie's veranda barely sheltered from a lashing rain that seems more like the falls of some vast equatorial river than anything the sky could send. Comforted only by a cup of iced Bud Lite, I struggle to breathe the still air. Great drops of sweat splotch these pages as I wonder about Maugham's story.

Did Sadie Thompson really exist? Did a fallen missionary really die here by his own hand? Does this building really have any place in history?

I don't know. But, in the face of those and of life's other many vagaries, I am consoled that I do know at least one immutable crystalline Truth: Somerset Maugham saw the rains of Pago Pago.

No one could make this up!

Chapter Fifteen
By Gravel Boat Through the Grenadines

The bartender at our hotel in Clifton, Union Island, St. Vincent and the Grenadines, told my wife and me that he knew the captain of the gravel hauling boat that was moored nearby at the island's main quay alongside the ferry-mail boat, "Barracouda." This wasn't surprising. Clifton is a small town, on a small island, in a small country, in the middle of the Caribbean Sea. Why shouldn't our rum-giver know the gravel boat captain?

Clifton is a quiet, out-of-the-way place with a certain backwater West Indian charm. A small, lean-to mountainside beer bar overlooks the tiny harbor. A few quite good cafeteria-style Caribbean restaurants dish out fried fish, plantains and pumpkin curry. A couple of basic, but adequate, hotels provide narrow beds and mosquito nets. About a dozen art and trinket shops cluster around the harbor, but they offer nothing like the tourist trap clutter of the cruise ship ports.

In short, Clifton ain't St. Thomas. But, if you are cruising the Caribbean on public boats, like we were, Clifton is an essential way station between the popular tourist islands of Grenada and Bequia. Over a few rums, we had told our bartender that, following the advice of The Lonely Planet Guide, we were taking a mail, cargo, and passenger vessel, the

"Barracouda," north to Kingston on St. Vincent Island early the following morning. From Kingston we would catch a smaller ferry back south to Bequia.

"The gravel boat sails directly to Bequia," our bartender said. "'Barracouda' bypasses Bequia and sails to Kingston. Not convenient for you. I'll go ask my friend, the Captain, to take you." And off he went. A few minutes later, he returned with the news: "Captain says you can come. No charge for my friends," he said as he reloaded our glasses. "Ship sail at 6:30 tomorrow morning."

And so began our gravel boat journey among the Grenadines' yacht-filled anchorages and islet havens of the mega-rich. Our vessel, "Joshua," had unloaded tons of dirt and gravel onto Clifton's small quay throughout the night before our departure. No one needed to tell us this because our hotel bedroom window was insufficient to the task of blocking the groans of hydraulic front-end loaders filling and refilling a phalanx of dump trucks and the ringing concussion of steel plate smashing concrete as each fully loaded truck raced off the ship's ramp onto the quay and into the inky darkness of an un-illuminated Clifton night.

Six-thirty was about the same time the "Joshua" finished noisily discharging her earthen cargo. We awoke to the sudden startling silence, and we stumbled unwashed and coffee-less to the dock. There, we discovered that the "Barracouda" had blocked the "Joshua's" departure while she boarded her passengers with the usual Caribbean sense of urgency.

We stowed our luggage in one of "Joshua's" lifeboats. Then my wife seized upon this unexpected delay as an opportunity to find coffee, even though the "Joshua's" crew had told us they would shove off immediately after the "Barracouda" embarked. And even though Clifton isn't exactly Seattle when it comes to finding coffee shops.

No sooner had she disappeared from sight, predictably, the "Barracouda" loaded its last passengers, cranked up its engines and threw off its mooring lines. About a minute later a helpful crewman told me: "We late. When the mail boat clear, Captain leave. With your wife or not, mon." Just then I spotted the distant speck of a woman holding two cups of coffee jogging toward us. When she saw me jumping and waving, she accelerated as fast as she could with her steaming burden. She reached us just as the crew began to pull up the ramp.

As we chugged into the waters of the Windward Islands, we surveyed our surroundings while savoring our thoroughly sloshed coffees. The "Joshua" was built in Pireaus, Greece a long time ago. She had probably spent her prior life redistributing Aegean gravel. On her immense forward deck, the trucks that had entertained us so well the previous night stood silent in neat rows. Aft, on the upper deck, the crew's lounge had a black and white TV that received only cricket broadcasts. The cooking galley posted the notice "Cook and Captain Only!" Above it all was the bridge and the Captain's quarters. He was a strong-looking, no-nonsense man. He wore a heavy gold chain against his bare ebony chest. The handwritten sign on his cabin door said it all: "DON'T EVEN THINK ABOUT OPENING THIS DOOR!"

We didn't open his door. Instead, we found a bench in the lounge and settled in for some cricket watching and for what we assumed would be a short trip to Bequia. We based our assumption on the deeply flawed predicate that since "Joshua" had already unloaded her colossal gravel cargo in Clifton, she was now simply returning to her home port.

We discovered our mistake about half an hour later when the Captain slowed us into a cove on Mayreau Island, just north of Union. One of the crew debarked and waded through the surf to secure our bowline to a boulder. Then the truck and loader drivers, who had been snoozing in their vehicles, started their engines, descended the ramp, and began to dig up Mayreau.

This hard work, exacerbated by the rising sun and heat, seemed to take hours. When the truck crew finally finished digging, loading and dumping, and the boat crew shoved "Joshua" off this now dirt-depleted island, we figured we were at last on our way to Bequia. However, when the Captain again reduced speed as Canouan Island came into view and drivers climbed back into their machines, we knew we were in for a seriously long day.

They were transferring all this dirt to Bequia. They moved so much dirt that by the time they had finished, the drivers had to park their machines on top of the mountain of it that covered the deck. They moved so much dirt that you might imagine, as you squinted through the mid-day glare at their frenzied digging, that they were pursuing some manic long-term scheme to relocate these islands to other parts of the Atlantic Ocean. The only island we passed that they didn't dig up was Mustique, which was probably exempt in deference to the reclusive rock stars and royalty who hide out there.

We eventually arrived at Bequia just before nightfall. After the tricky start with my wife juggling coffees and sprinting for a moving boat, everyone on the "Joshua," including the Captain, was friendly to us. The cook let my wife (but not me) into the forbidden galley to help her prepare a very good curry lunch. During a quiet moment, the Captain let us pass through the "Enter and Die" door and onto the bridge. And, crucially, he arranged for a jeep to meet us at his mooring in Bequia and drive us across the island to our hotel.

When we reached our hotel, we met travelers who had made the journey from Union to Bequia via Kingston on the "Barracouda." They were already deep into cocktail hour.

But we had a better story.

Chapter Sixteen
Captivating Cape Verde
Locked in an African Wine Bar

I'm sitting in an African bar scratching a description of Praia, Cape Verde, into a notebook, sipping my third cup of passable Portuguese plonk. I don't know if it was my intense concentration on the composition, or the fact that I'd asked for the third cup of wine after the staff had already switched off the lights and bolted the door, but something clued the owner that I might be a travel writer. He has just introduced himself and handed me the card of his humble but friendly establishment.

I conclude that this gentleman has never met a real travel writer because I neither asked the waitress to leave the jug, nor checked their cupboards for extra bottles. The fact that he didn't refill my cup when he proffered his card leads me to further conclude that he doesn't know how to get good copy out of a real travel writer, should he ever meet one.

Anyway, prior to this minor distraction, I was preparing to report that "de rigueur" rusted harbour-side cannon barrels overlook the listing skeletons of wrecked ships stuck in the oozy sand of Praia's…umm…praia. And that the beach itself is the color of brown beer bottles, which is not surprising considering the colossal number of empty Sagres beer bottles left there to decompose.

The upside to this alarming environmental news is that in this arid town with less grass than a putting green, where the afternoon air approaches the temperature recommended for baking a turkey, where the Sahara's dust finally settles after its long journey from Mauritania, you are never far from a cold one.

Praia became the capital of this West African archipelago, formerly part of the Portuguese empire, after Francis Drake sacked the original capital, Ribeira Grande, in 1585.

Cape Verde fell into economic obscurity in the 19th century with the decline of the whaling industry, and after Abolition ended its infamous role as a market and transit station in the horrific Atlantic slave trade.

Since the appellation "green" has about as much relevance to Cape Verde as it does to Greenland, the prospects for an agricultural society were hopeless. Deadly drought followed deadly drought. Survivors fled to Massachusetts, Brazil and Lisbon. They left behind a few hearty souls to create a unique music style, to insanely celebrate the football successes of Benfica and Sporting Lisbon, and to conduct extensive research into the biodegradable characteristics of beer bottles.

If you ever find yourself in Praia without the good fortune of being confined in a bar with a seemingly endless supply of cheap *vinho tinto*, I recommend a trip across the interior of Praia's island, Santiago. Santiago is about the size and shape of Barbados, but without grass, palm trees, steel bands, dark rum, or powdery white beaches sprawling with topless tourists.

My guidebook tells me that with the help of the usual suspects: UN, US and EU, Cape Verde has undertaken a massive re-forestation effort using a "species of acacia tree particularly adapted to the area's conditions." The day before I got locked in this wine cellar, I took that trip, and all I can say for certain is that this species of acacia tree is particularly adapted to catching and holding the millions of multicoloured plastic bags passing motorists launch across the rubbled roadside. Some particularly well-adapted trees were adorned with as many as ten sacks flapping in the dusty breeze like a Chinese banner ceremony.

The trip across Santiago to the northern town of Tarrafal took three hours through landscape I would call "lunar" but I would be maligning the moon. Despite this agricultural handicap, the irrepressible Cape Verdeans have contrived to summon enough water from the earth and collect enough rainfall every year or so to cultivate occasional patches of mango, banana and sugar cane. The sugar cane they distil into a beverage called "grogo," which will shut down your synapses before you can say, "Damn! This shit tastes strong!"

But left to its own devices, the land would yield nothing but dust and cactus. More remarkable than the stark landscape, are the pastel stucco dwellings that appear to have been airlifted from the Algarve and set down on the high slopes of rocky pathless pinnacles.

I asked my driver how these people managed to exist up there and he logically pointed out that there was a grocery store only a few kilometres walk away.

We passed this shop on our descent into Tarrafal. While it wasn't Whole Foods, it did have sufficient survival rations and even a few luxury goods, like tins of imported olive oil and chorizos. Where those mountain people conjured up the money to buy these goodies, though, is anybody's guess.

When we arrived in Tarrafal, I learned that the main "tourist attraction" is the ruins of former dictator, Antonio Salazar's, concentration camp for Portuguese and African political prisoners. Anyone who has ever seen an abandoned concentration camp would never mistake this place, with its barrier ditches, barbed wire and gun towers, for anything else. One wartime writer observed that the only difference between Dachau and Tarrafal was that Dachau was ruled by "General Winter" while Tarrafal was ruled by "General Summer." Hot, Dry, Airless, Savage, fall far short of describing the horror that would have been this prison.

Beyond that sobering site, the village has a small clean cove of a beach and a seaside terrace for eating freshly grilled fish and swallowing icy Sagres. Nice as it was, we couldn't linger long over lunch. We had to hurry back to Praia. Benfica v. Sporting was kicking off early.

As I finish this article, chance has it that the friendly owner is ready to unlock the door to admit the first of the dinner trade and release me into another Praia evening, before he rushes to replenish his wine supply.

Europe

Chapter Seventeen
A Personal Train Through Transylvania

"The painfully slow Personal trains should be avoided as a rule, unless you're heading for some tiny destination." The Rough Guide to Romania

"These trains are achingly slow." Lonely Planet Guide Eastern Europe

I hadn't sufficiently studied my guidebooks when I asked the lady in the Brasov, Romania Tourist Information office for the train times to Sighisoara, the birthplace and family home of national hero, Vlad the Impaler (AKA Dracula).

"The Intercity trains to Sighisoara depart at 10:36 and 15:45," she told me.

"But I want to leave around noon," I said.

"I am afraid that only a Personal train leaves around noon," she said. "We never recommend for the foreign tourist to travel by Personal train."

Duly warned, but committed to my schedule, I approached the Brasov station ticket counter the next day and requested a ticket on the Personal train to

Sighisoara. "First Class or Second Class?" The agent asked. When I learned that the price difference was only 7 Romanian Lei (about $3), I splurged for the best, assuming that the discomforts the Personal train could be assuaged by an upgrade.

I bought a sack of Romanian beer from the platform kiosk as an additional precaution and sat down to wait for my Personal train. At nearly the appointed hour, a small diesel engine towing half a dozen carriages that may have once been painted blue with windows that may have once been transparent staggered onto the designated platform.

I searched each car's markings but saw no first-class compartments. This omission, coupled with the fact that the train's final destination was not Sighisoara, led me to conclude that this was someone else's Personal train, not mine. But when all my fellow platform occupants boarded, I took the precautionary step of showing the conductor my ticket emphasizing the prominent "1" next to the word *"Clase"* and with a perplexed look, pointed at the train.

Then I learned a simple but important Romanian train travel truth: Even though a ticket agent will gladly sell you a First-Class ticket on a Personal train, this sale in no way implies that the train actually carries a First-Class compartment.

The conductor found great humor in my revelation. He laughed, *"Da, Da.* Is train. Is train," and gave me a hand up as the train started to move. By the look of the conductor's oil-stained uniform and haggard face, I guessed he rarely finds humor in his work and was consoled to have given him the light-hearted moment that only a clueless foreign traveler can provide.

As the train left Brasov and its personal passengers began to unscrew their liters of brown beer, unwrap their packages of sweaty salami and pull off their shoes, I knew I was, at least, getting the real Transylvania travel experience. If this train had had a first-class compartment, I would have surely been its only occupant.

Still, I was out 7 Lei, and when the ticket checker came by, I attempted to alert her to this injustice. She responded in English with words she must have memorized when previously confronted with First Class foreigners on the Personal train: "I am sorry."

"So can I have a 7 Lei refund?"

"I am sorry."

"This is no way to run a railroad."

"I am sorry." She emphasized for the last time as she moved on to check the Second-Class tickets and I decided to abandon my grievance and crack open a brown beer. "When in Romania…" as they say.

The train's bench seats were either designed in the style of a 1950's American school bus or stolen from a 1950's American school bus. They were covered in the hide of a long dead creature that may have once been brown. The windows, though smeared and sooty, were functional for countryside viewing and for savagely increasing the late spring's afternoon temperatures on the sun side of the train.

My bench-mate fellow traveler was a quiet rural gent who occasionally chewed on something that looked like meat. He was dressed in an olive-green sweater that needed some darning and a black wool coat that would have kept him warm through a Carpathian winter but was dangerously inappropriate for a window seat on the sun side of the train. He had fastened a strip of ribbon in the national colors to his lapel as a kind of do-it-yourself flag pin.

I imagined his name was Gheorghe and he had suffered under Nicolae Ceausecu's agricultural collectivization disaster. He looked about the right age to have lost everything when Communists confiscated small private farms but looked too old to have started over after the 1989 Revolution. He nodded sympathetically when the ticket checker expressed her sorrow at my worthless first-class ticket, but he was otherwise a non-communicative companion.

We had only traveled about 10 miles when I discovered the significance of the term "personal" train. I had originally assumed that it was some translation mistake by the Brasov Tourist Information lady. But no. Personal train passengers can make the train stop anywhere they personally want.

If they want to stop in front of their farmhouse, at a fishing pond, or beside a sports field, they tell the conductor, and the train stops to let them off. At these personal stops there are no platforms. The passengers just jump down onto the ground with their sack of feed, their fishing rod, or their football and pick their way across the tracks to their own personal destination.

The Personal train traveler gets a close view of Transylvanian country life. Horse-drawn plows furrow rich soil. Strong well-fed men in white shirts and suspenders cut hay with a scythe, rake it by hand,

and load it onto horse-drawn wagons. Women gather at communal roadside hand pumps to collect water. Children in bright clothes scurry everywhere.

Personal trains do make scheduled stops at tiny villages with tiny station houses and platforms, but passengers mostly get on the train there, not off. If your destination is a scheduled stop, presumably, you don't take the Personal train.

Personal train passengers enjoy curling up on the hard benches after overdosing on brown beer and sausage. Since most of these guys are soon snoring away, and since the conductor makes no stop announcements, I deduced that a designated "stay-awake-passenger" system is employed to arouse these Un-Dead from their slumber at the correct disembarkation point.

I had designated no one to wake me, and Gheorghe looked fairly unreliable, so I tried to stay alert. This proved difficult in the slow moving, gently swaying, overly warm carriage that smelled like a deli. To make matters worse, I assumed, after watching the train's randomly interrupted progress, that the "Arrival Time" printed on my ticket was just a space filler.

Somehow, I stayed awake or jolted awake, and incredibly, we pulled into Sighisoara within 5 minutes of "On Time," albeit long after a regular train would have arrived. Experience, luck, or sophisticated computer modeling of decades of Personal train disembarkation data must have assisted this scheduling miracle.

However they did it, I was impressed with the punctuality, amused by my fellow personal travelers, and most importantly, after a massive wreck the day before on a Romanian Intercity train, happy to be safely delivered to my destination.

I only wished I had my 7 Lei back.

Chapter Eighteen
Portugal's Stonehenge

In Portugal's southern Alentejo province, near the town of Evora, in the incongruous midst of a vast cork plantation, stands Portugal's Stonehenge. It is called Os Almendres. Around six thousand years ago, for no obvious reason, the inhabitants of this arid inland plateau interrupted their hunting and gathering activities to somehow drag nearly 100 gigantic granite stones, to a sloping dusty mound. They planted them vertically in roughly concentric circles and in a discernible, but inexplicable, sequence of heights.

The cork plantation the stones now stand among enhances the otherworldliness of the scene. Cork trees are gnarled and bent with small but abundant olive-drab leaves. A recently harvested one looks as much like a clipped French poodle as a tree can. Its lower trunk is shaved bald, but its top has thick gray furry bark and bushy foliage. Virtually no ground vegetation surrounds these trees.

If you travel the 12 miles from Evora to Almendres, you are at first stunned by how difficult it would have been for such an early civilisation to move these stones. But then, almost immediately, you confront a set of imponderable questions: "What were these people thinking? How could this have possibly been a worthwhile use of their limited resources?"

I am writing this in a pleasant Evora café near the ruins of a Roman temple while I recover from my visit to Almendres with a glass of Alentejo vinho branco. Around me sit several descendants of that curious rock-moving tribe. These particular descendants show no signs of putting down their espressos and beers to go look for really heavy stones to carry up a hill. That is not, however, to imply that they back down from other extraordinary challenges like consuming large steaks, boiled potatoes, fried eggs, sliced tomatoes, and lots of red wine at a mid-week summer lunch.

But I digress from the original question: Why are those rocks on that mound? Since every unanswerable question deserves a definitive answer, archaeologists, theologians, astronomers, anthropologists, and sex therapists have labored for years to provide one or more definitive answers.

Some of the various hypotheses are: The ancients arranged the stones in circles to help themselves observe astronomical movements so they could anticipate seasonal changes that would tell them when to plant their crops, organise their parties, or set their clocks to savings time.

Or they shaved the tops off some of the stones to form a flat surface suitable for animal, vegetable or human sacrifices to appease the Necessaries to send rain, or game to hunt, or a successful football season, if the area's current inhabitants' passions are any indication.

Or they selected certain stones for their phallic shape. It takes no Freudian analyst to see how one special stone could become a persuasive new product logo for Viagra. Therefore, the rock-laying people must have conducted fertility rites or Ibiza-style rave-ups during those ancient evenings.

All these reasons, and others, are possible. But whatever the reason, or lack of reason, for this rock moving enthusiasm, Almendres makes a nice counterpoint to Stonehenge. No fences or guards regulate access to the Almendres stones because no one wants to paint ARSENAL RULES on them. No tea rooms, souvenir shops, or tour coaches disturb their tranquillity because they aren't world famous, and they aren't off the M 3. And at the solstice, no white-clad Druids dance around them proclaiming the New World because the Portuguese just don't do that religion.

In conclusion, if you appreciate the special aura of Stonehenge despite the drawbacks of excessive tourism and other modern manias, then you should make the relatively short trip to Almendres the next time you find yourself in Lisbon with two days to spare. If you do, you will stand in the hot still air of the dusty Alentejo plain, inside those timeless circles of systematically placed megalithic stones, surrounded by an eerie gray-green expanse of cork forest, and you will quietly wonder: "Why did they do it?"

Postscript

The day after my visit to Os Almendres, I took a tour to a cave where these prehistoric rock-moving people may once have lived. There, our guide began to explain that in the unimaginable distant past some evolving human picked up a sharp-edged stone and scratched a fragile, but perfectly realized image of a running horse with a flowing mane on the wall of this lightless Iberian alcove.

Suddenly, the guide frantically shrieked: "Idiota! No touch the wall!" as a Canadian tourist in a Hard Rock T-shirt rubbed his oily finger across the horse's mane.

Waiting for the Ferry

Sunday cathedral chimes loudly
intrude upon the late afternoon
Andalusian café.
An old man, not dirty,
but leathered and bent
and wearing broken shoes
can't sell the patrons
any of his worthless trinkets.
Waived off and ignored
he picks up the plastic sack
of his entire estate
and walks toward the sunset.

The church bells relent.
The waiters bring coffees.
The ferry back to Portugal embarks.

Chapter Nineteen
Lundy Island
North Devon's Puffin Hangout

It seemed like a great stroke of luck when I booked the last two tickets available on the M.S. Oldenberg from Bideford, North Devon to Lundy Island on a high season Saturday. That is until I discovered I had booked tickets number 266 and 267 on a vessel built for the post-war German railroad and apparently designed for far fewer passengers.

This would still have been all right if about fifty of our fellow travelers had not comprised a boy scout troop who had been filled to the gunwales with chocolate ice cream just before we hit eight-foot swells in the Bristol Channel. After a few minutes of Oldenberg exhaust and what looked like a group try out for the bedroom scene in "The Exorcist," I wasn't feeling too well myself and went downstairs to try to concentrate on the horizon and ignore the scouts.

Fortunately, most good boat rides eventually do end and after a little over two hours, ours ended in the calmer anchorage of Lundy. Lundy is a 3 by 1 mile speck of moor-covered granite off the coast of North Devon. It has a permanent population of about twelve, but annually pulls in some 20,000 day-trippers like the scouts and me and a thousand or so "stayers" who can overnight in anything from a campground to a castle or a lighthouse.

Because landings at both ends of the journey must be made at high tide, the length of stay on day trips is variable. Ours was five hours, which was long enough to organise my Devonian wife onto a route march in her Italian loafers to search for puffins at the northern tip of the island.

We made the distance only because we followed the admonition of an experienced Lundy day-tripper: "Don't stop at Marisco's Tavern as soon as you land." In our case this advice was even easier to follow than normal since the tavern was being used as a staging area for scout cleaning when we arrived.

Marisco's Tavern and the remnants of nearby Marisco's Castle take their name from the clan that operated the island in the 12th and 13th centuries for the profitable businesses of smuggling, piracy, plundering shipwrecks, and raiding the mainland. These enterprises thrived until around 1250 when one William Marisco, after being arrested for plotting to assassinate King Henry III, earned the distinction of becoming the first prisoner to be hanged, drawn and quartered under English justice. To add insult to injury, the Crown then confiscated his land holdings, including, of course, the pirate lair of Lundy.

The island takes its name from the Old Norse word for puffin— "lund." These pandas of the bird world nest here by the thousands and they are the principal attraction for any visitor who ventures out of Marisco's Tavern. The birds are so identified with the place that Lundy issues postage stamps denominated in "Puffins."

Besides the castle and tavern, the settlement has an old, whitewashed lighthouse that's often shrouded in mist and a nineteenth century church named St. Helen's, which is large enough for all of Lundy's residents and their extended families for at least four generations.

The island's main shop is on the road out of the settlement just past the small campground. Here my wife and I loaded up on snacks and water for our expedition. We began walking along the western windward side. At Lundy's western edge, the land descends almost vertically from the turfy green plateau down three hundred feet of granite cliffs to the ocean.

The relentless surf has carved the cliffs into odd formations with descriptive names like The Pyramid, The Cheeses, Needle Rock, Devil's Chimney, which are popular with serious rock climbers. The sea surges high here and just offshore on the outcropped rocks, seals bob in the foam.

The north-south path across Lundy is segmented by stonewalls, which serve as crowd control for the island's sheep and goats. These walls have the logical, but inaccurate names of Quarter Wall, Halfway Wall and Three-Quarter Wall. But as my wife casually observed, "That Three-Quarter Wall is a hell of a long way from the end, and just look at the state of these shoes!" Between the walls, hundreds of longhaired goats and the occasional sika deer munch heather, flowers, and discarded apple cores.

Upon reaching the northern point, the fortunate tourist can be rewarded with the sight of nesting puffins. We were not. Puffin nesting is a seasonal activity. But our consolation was a high sea vista narrated by eerie moaning seal cries echoing off an amphitheatre of the cliffs.

It was indeed a contemplative place, but with the tide returning, we had to contemplate the Oldenberg, and we started back along the calmer eastern shore. What few people have lived on Lundy in the past, mainly lived on the eastern side.

At the far north-eastern end, completely remote from mankind is the ruined stone bungalow of a thoroughly anti-social individual. Closer to the current settlements are abandoned quarries and abandoned cottages of abandoned quarry workers. Slightly off the path, near Quarter Wall, is a small poignant memorial to a Lundy resident killed in action in Burma on Easter, 1944.

Back through Quarter Wall and into the metropolis again, we had just enough time for a quick pint a Marisco's while examining what seven miles of soggy moor can do to a pair of Italian designer shoes. The pub is a welcome refuge from the wind, cold and mud. It is decorated with maps and mementos of the hundreds of ships that have wrecked off Lundy and with the flags and emblems of the Royal Lifeboat crews who have tried to rescue the survivors.

Beer is served by a cheery staff who seem to enjoy the island and wish short trippers could spend more time. Our time, however, was up and it was down to the ramps and on to our cruiser for what, happily for the scouts and me, proved to be a calm return voyage to Bideford.

Chapter Twenty
England's Eclipse 1999

"That's eet, then, is eet?" With that summation, the final total eclipse of the last millennium ended after 40 seconds under an overcast sky on Dartmoor for a young Manchester woman with two cranky kids. "I kood 'ave stayed at 'ome an' seen ninety percent of it. I'm absolutely gutted."

It was one opinion. But for the thousands of other people whose cars lined the road to Princeton for miles, who scrambled over the rocky tors, and among the sheep and ponies for the best views of…of clouds, it was surely a minority opinion. Because even without the sun, even without the Bailey's Beads, the "diamond ring" affect, the chromosphere, "eet" was a show. And if, like me, and my Devonian wife, you'd only traveled an hour from North Devon, without kids, it was well worth the trouble.

True, the thick cloud cover blocked out all sightings of the sun except a momentary apparition of a partial eclipse, which the crowd must have willed out of the gloom. From our hilltop perch it was like sitting under a gray galactic wok. But the minutes leading up to totality and the blackout itself stunned everyone, even silencing our gutted friend's children for an instant.

Most sun gazers had waited for hours. Some had camped. By ten o'clock, they had no hope of seeing the sun as thicker clouds moved in from the Atlantic. "Which way are we supposed to be looking?" someone asked. "I dunno, which way are the telescopes pointed?" was the helpful reply.

Without being able to watch the moon's path across the sun, we had to wait for twilight to know totality was approaching. The twilight came imperceptibly at first; but darkened rapidly over about ten minutes. The faint warmth of the winter morning vanished as the temperature jolted to freezing.

There was still plenty of light until precisely 11:13 a.m. when, just as the experts explained would happen, the western horizon went black. At first it was just a thin black streak against the edge of the moor. Then, suddenly, the blackness rushed east over our heads as if the light had been rolled up like a great celestial carpet. I was abruptly reminded of some verses of scripture: "In the Beginning was the Word, and the Word was: 'Crikey, Sylvia look at that!'…And Darkness was upon the Face of the Deep."

In the distant south, below us, the automatic streetlights of Plymouth switched on to outline the city and illuminate the English coast. Throughout the moor, hundreds of cameras flashed in a futile attempt to photograph, I dare say what. For a few seconds there was no sound but the brisk blackened wind over the grasses.

As soon as the crowd understood, without the aid of actually seeing the sun's corona, that we were in a total eclipse, the western horizon began to lighten again. In a few more seconds, the whole cloud cover turned a pale luminous colour of silver. It was a colour of sky I have previously seen only in advance of vast tornado fronts crossing the American plains. Then dawn broke. The natural dappled light of a cloudy English day resumed its rightful place to spontaneous applause and cheering across the moor. And God saw that it was good.

It took a few more minutes before people talked again. Then little by little, they began to shift themselves off the rocks and tramp back to the road to start their long motorcade up the moor lanes.

And then, that was eet.

Chapter Twenty-One
An English D-Day Remnant

An unlikely memorial to the D-Day invasion lies half hidden in a narrow wind-ravaged valley among the sand dunes of Braunton Burrows on the north coast of Devon, England. While the remembrance sites in France have become places of pilgrimage, this isolated spot in rural England is virtually unknown.

In September 1943, thousands of Allied troops began training here for the invasion of France. The troops encamped on the Burrows and on adjacent farmland and golf courses. They came here because the tidal reaches of the estuaries on this coast of England are similar to the conditions at Normandy.

The armies built roads, dug bunkers and trenches, and erected tent compounds. Old photos in the rebuilt golf club depict the frenetic activity of earthmovers, tanks and battalions of soldiers transforming the area into a vast training facility for the recapture of Europe.

Today, Braunton Burrows is again a pristine nature reserve. Golfers now crowd the rebuilt courses, while hikers clamber over the dunes, sheep graze the farmlands, and rabbits scurry through the grass. Little evidence remains of those desperate days except for four oddly aligned concrete slabs near a rough gravel track that locals still call "The American Road."

The strange slabs are not visible from either the beach or the American Road. No signposts mark their location. If you don't know where to look, you would be lucky to chance upon them, as I recently did.

I was walking along a high dune when I spotted what appeared to be miniature runways and climbed down to explore. The "runways" are flat rectangular pavements about 120 feet long and 35 feet wide lying in an overgrowth of scrub. Around the edges of each are rows of broken rusted posts and rings. At the front, two low concrete walls narrow onto a concrete ramp. The ramp descends into a trough of slimy green water.

In this incongruous setting, it took me a few moments to realize that I was standing on the deck of a simulated infantry landing craft and the stagnant water I was peering into was "Omaha Beach." The posts and rings must have supported the sides and stern of the "vessel."

Nearly eighty years ago, soldiers in full battle gear charged down that ramp through the trough and on to "France" in final preparations for June 6. For one vivid instant, I could almost see the ramp drop and machine gun fire riddle the front row.

When that awful image gave way again to the calming whir of insects and the cries of sea birds circling against the misty sky, I noticed an unobtrusive granite plaque on the forward wall. It simply reads: "IN COMMEMORATION OF THOSE MEMBERS OF THE ALLIED FORCES WHO TRAINED HERE FOR THE LIBERATION OF EUROPE, "D" DAY JUNE 6TH 1944."

And it silently reminds a few passers-by of those men's impending sacrifice and of another time when the world was not a secure or a peaceful place.

Chapter Twenty-Two
A Walk In West Belfast

[This article was written not long after eighteen months of picketing and violent, abusive protests surrounding the Holy Cross School access dispute in the Ardoyne district of Belfast culminated in a major riot in January 2002.]

In the late 1960's, Northern Ireland's Catholic leaders were inspired by the Civil Rights movement in the United States to confront the Protestant-Unionist establishment to obtain equality in housing and economic opportunities. They staged sit-ins and marches that provoked violent responses from both security officials and civilians. There was even a long march from Belfast to Derry, which was repulsed at a bridge crossing reminiscent of the pivotal Selma to Montgomery march. These peaceful protests and violent responses covered by the British media, eventually resulted in London's intervention to compel the Protestant controlled Belfast government to make concessions toward more equal treatment of the Catholic minority.

Unfortunately, there was an ancient and more ominous conflict than equal treatment before the law still smouldering. It was the Catholic's struggle for a unified Irish republic and the final ouster of the

British from their island against the northern Protestant Loyalist's defiant refusal to be absorbed into the Catholic majority nation of Ireland. This eventually overtook the non-violent civil rights movement of the early days and led to savagery and terror on both sides of the Irish Sea for 30 years until the cease-fire and power-sharing "Good Friday Agreement" of 1998.

Although the power sharing agreements are currently threatened by allegations of IRA espionage and London's consequent suspension of the Ulster Parliament, the cease-fire has, nevertheless, so far eliminated organized militia warfare. Despite occasional individual acts of violence, life in most of Belfast has now achieved comparative normalcy. Some sections of the city, however, are less "normal" than others, and West Belfast, the home of Gerry Adams, is one of those.

I went to West Belfast this summer before the latest political crisis. As an American southerner, who grew up in Alabama in the 1950's and 60's, during the era of racial segregation, discrimination, and systematic voter suppression, I was interested in the different paths the two contemporaneous civil rights movements had taken.

Two main thoroughfares run through West Belfast. Shankhill Road is Protestant. The Falls Road is Catholic. They are only a few hundred yards apart and are connected by cross streets, which during the worst of "The Troubles," were blocked by 15-foot-high steel "Peace Walls" to keep the communities separated. Even today, the black share-cabs in this area drive separate parallel routes. Protestant-driven cabs ply Shankhill, Catholic-driven cabs the Falls. To get from one district to the other using these cabs, you need to ride all the way to the edge of central Belfast where the two routes terminate, get out, switch cabs and ride back.

Shankhill and the Falls Road are neighborhoods with Attitude. On Shankhill, Union Jacks, Red Hand of Ulster flags, and the flags of the previously violent militia fly from every street lamppost. Curbsides are painted British red, white and blue. Vast murals on the walls of housing blocks and shop buildings depict every aspect of the Ulster Protestants' long fight, from the ancient victories of Oliver Cromwell and William of Orange to the recent imprisonment of murderous militiamen like Johnny "Mad Dog" Adair, "His Only Crime Was Loyalty." While on the Falls Road, the murals decry police and army violence against Catholics and commemorate their martyrs, like Bobby Sands.

I started walking up Shankhill at about lunchtime. I was heading toward the Catholic enclave of the Ardoyne, where last year, Catholic schoolgirls had to walk a gauntlet of jeering Protestant crowds to take the shortest route to their school through Protestant territory.

I hadn't gone far when a sudden Irish rainstorm drove me into a Loyalist pub for refuge. Inside, the pub's allegiance was clear. To fit more Union Jacks across the ceiling or more pictures of the Queen along the walls, they would have needed to build an extension. Around the edge of the bar old men in cloth caps huddled around their Guinness and watched the History Channel on TV. The place would have probably been a "legitimate target" in the seventies, but that day, it seemed no more provocative than an English pub that backs a particular football club.

Approaching the bar, I remembered the advice of my English brother-in-law: "Make sure they immediately know you're an American tourist. You'll be a neutral and have no problems in either community." It worked: "Right Yank. Would that be a Guinness?" the bartender asked.

With my status confirmed, a pleasant, rather one-sided conversation ensued. "How are you liking our Belfast sunshine? What are you interested to see here? Yes, that's right, Gerry Adams is our MP. No, I can't believe it either. Don't think he likes it any more than we."

When I told the bartender I was heading up to the Ardoyne, he said, "I've lived here for forty years, and I've never been there. Maybe one day I'll put on a camera and a backpack like you and go up to see it." I promised to report back as I walked out into the slackening drizzle.

Less than two miles separate my loyalist pub on lower Shankhill from the Ardoyne. The route passes an Orange Lodge, the Official Northern Ireland Football Supporters Club, and a number of "souvenir shops" with catchy names like "One Island, Two Nations" where you can "Buy all of your Loyalist needs."

At the end of Shankhill, the road heads uphill and bends right. That's where I got my first glimpse of the Irish green, white and orange tricolor flags (some with the orange stripe ripped off) flying just as defiantly as the Unionist flags had flown a few blocks down the road. Between the two districts, the "invisible line," ironically named Alliance Street, bore the signs of a failed demilitarized zone with shattered glass and hurled paint decorating the pavement.

Beyond Alliance Street, however, in the daylight at least, the rest of the neighborhoods seemed like placid, quiet inner suburbs with an odd penchant for politics. You would have difficulty remembering this was a place of random murders, car bombs, firebombs, drive-by shootings, rock-throwing demonstrations, and police charges into rioting mobs. But that day, they were communities of red brick terrace houses with neat front gardens and small bay windows displaying cute bric-a-brac next to their "No Surrender" posters.

On the Catholic Ardoyne side of Alliance, just as my bartender had foreseen, two women passed me and cheerily observed: "You MUST be a tourist." A little further on, the geographical situation that had precipitated the jeering assaults on the schoolgirls became obvious. There is no direct way to walk from the small enclave of the Ardoyne to their school without crossing the territory of a Protestant neighborhood that displayed even more symbols of partisan Unionism than Shankhill itself. Marching, or in their case simply walking, through rival territory has long been provocative here.

But that day, nothing was happening. It was a little boring, it was uphill, and it was raining again, so I turned around. Walking back, I noticed, on the Catholic side of the border zone, an enormous black and white mural proclaiming the school accesses grievance in simple terms that were especially evocative to an American southerner. On the left half of the mural were a group of white adults shouting abuse and black school children. On the right half was a terrified Catholic girl cowering against shouting Protestants. The caption read: "Arkansas 1957. Ardoyne 1999. Human Rights. Its Black and White."

So the American Civil Rights Movement is still an inspirational theme for Northern Ireland's minority 45 years after it essentially began at Little Rock's Central High School and more than 30 years after it achieved the goal of legal equality in the States. Pondering this revelation, I wandered back to my favorite Shankhill pub. The friendly barman handed me a Guinness and asked, "What did ye think of the Ardoyne, then?"

I said, "They really seem a lot like you people down here."

"Nay, lad," he said. "That's where you'd be wrong."

I finished my walk through a newly opened "Peace Wall" to the Falls Road where I caught a Catholic share cab. We drove past Irish flags, murals of black-hooded gunmen, and the spray-painted slogans of the Republican militants: "Never Forget Never Forget Never Forget."

By the time we reached the Central district, I knew the Shankhill barman's opinion was wrong. The two West Belfast communities do have much in common. But that, in many ways, is the bad news.

Chapter Twenty-Three
The Queen's Golden Jubilee

[Compared to mood of the 2022 Platinum Jubilee, which despite the pomp, was subdued by concerns about the Queen's failing health, the Golden Jubilee, a quarter century before, was a full-on national party.]

My 75-year-old next-door neighbor in Devon, England, Mrs. Yeo, recently leaned over our garden wall and announced that she had just returned from paying her final respects to the late Queen Mother in London.

"My brother picked me up before dawn and we drove for five hours. We stood in queue for seven hours to get into the chapel. After we left the chapel, we found the car and drove back."

"That sounds like an awfully long day," I said.

"It has to be done, hasn't it? She said.

"So, how often do you get up to London, Mrs. Yeo?"

"Last time was the Silver Jubilee in '77."

"That would make around four times a century, then?"

"Guess that's about right. I only go if it's important."

Mrs. Yeo's view is pretty consistent with the attitude of many traditional people in this conservative part of England's West Country. They respect the monarchy (especially the Queen and Queen Mother), but they have little use for their nation's capital.

This put the countryside people in a bit of a quandary when it came to this year's Golden Jubilee celebrations. Although the Queen is touring the whole of the United Kingdom, including Northern Ireland, for the Jubilee, most of the official Jubilee functions from June 1-4 were held in London.

She hosted a Classical Concert and a Pop Concert at Buckingham Palace, attended a Jubilee Festival with Prince Philip on Pall Mall, and culminated the long weekend with a procession to St Paul's where a National Thanksgiving Service was held.

These events were planned in the minutest detail: "Her Majesty and The Duke of Edinburgh will arrive at 19:43…." They were carried off with all the colour, splendour, and RAF fly-bys that a thousand-year tradition of monarchy can bring to a televised social occasion. Millions thronged the roads and the parks. It was fantastic, if you were in London. But I'm pretty sure Mrs. Yeo wouldn't go to the Palace and sing "All You Need Is Love" with Paul McCartney and Eric Clapton. Even if she had had an invitation, she'd already used up her quota of London visits for the next 25 years.

So how do rural English people show their loyalty, feel part of such national celebrations, and still stay home? The British solution to this problem for everything from coronations to V-E Day to jubilees has long been the local "Street Party." Don't let the name deceive you. Over the years, a traditional English village Street Party has had little to do with kegs of beer and even less to do with amplified rock music. The featured beverage was usually tea served with cakes and sandwiches, on long tables decorated with everything you can fashion from a Union Jack. A school band played, songs were sung, parades paraded.

Children have always been the main focus of these gatherings. The idea is to give them a sense of occasion and history at seminal national events. They usually receive those souvenir ceramic cups and other curios that often find their way into the shops along Portobello Road after languishing for decades in attics and cellars.

The adult-oriented segment of a Street Party, which would include the previously mentioned kegs of beer, took place off the street in a local Hound and Trumpet after the kids were finally rounded up and wiped down. It was good homey family fun, to be sure, but is it still relevant in 21st century Britain?

At Queen Elizabeth's Silver Jubilee, around 5000 towns and villages held Street Party celebrations. They were a source of civic pride. Their organization would have occupied parish committees and officials for months. But this time things appeared to be different. Far fewer places planned street parties this year. This fact was deduced because local organizers were requested to register with a Central Jubilee Commission. The Commission even published a Toolkit for party planning on the Internet.

The Toolkit followed a nine-month timeline for preparations with appropriate checklists. It included helpful advice on how to set up a beer tent and thoughtful tips like don't put the toddler's play area next to the beer tent. Public convenience was also addressed: allow one toilet for every 50 female guests. As was public safety: always consult the Civil Aviation Authority before setting off fireworks next to an airport runway. All valuable information, no doubt, but one sensed that a little of the exuberant spontaneity of previous times had been lost.

The national newspapers ran features earlier this year on the tradition of street party celebrations. They observed that today's England is so different from 25 years ago that such events are now probably anachronistic. Therefore, not many were planned despite the advent of the Toolkit.

Certainly, the black and white photographs and home movies of the Silver Jubilee celebrations support the newspapers' view. Images of ladies in floral dresses and sturdy shoes, men in dark suits and ties, and children in school uniforms frantically waving little flags recall a more innocent time, like America in the early Fifties.

A few months ago, if you'd asked most Englishmen what important event was scheduled for the first weekend in June, you'd have likely heard, "First round of the World Cup, mate. England v. Sweden, isn't it?" But, following the Queen Mother's funeral services with the astounding outpouring of public affection for her and with the onset of the televised pageantry of preliminary Jubilee events, the mood seemed to shift. This is an important symbolic year for the British. The notion that something must be done gained momentum.

Our little village and many others decided to hold parties, and ours was slightly irreverent. Discarding the Toolkit, our celebrations were opened by a regally attired drag "Queen." Inexplicably escorted by a man in a toga wearing a Roman helmet, "she" strutted behind a bagpipe corps through festooned cobbled lanes alongside ancient cottages draped in bunting to the church square. Crowds of normally sensible adults wearing plastic union jack bowlers with red, white and blue tinsel wigs and face-painted children flapping hundreds of little flags cheered her on.

Arriving at the square to sound of church bells peeling and speakers blaring "Mustang Sally" across the estuary, our Queen declared the festivities open at the appointed hour of 3:00 p.m. Then, exhausted from the burdens of office, she lay down her wig and crown (heavy is the head), loosened her dress, and retired to The Royal George for a rejuvenating gin (God save her). The rest of the crowd made for the sagging tables of country food. The party raged well into the night and culminated with a fireworks display, set off, presumably, at the prescribed distance from the nearest airport runway.

A time traveler from the Silver Jubilee may have been shocked by our parade. She would have been stunned by the differences in dress and music styles, in lighting and sound systems, in portable toilet technology, but she would have happily recognized all the little flags and she would have clearly understood the prevailing mood of it all...

"It has to be done, hasn't it?"

America

Chapter Twenty-Four
Bordering On Lunacy

A Taxi Tour in the Mexican Borderlands

Ciudad Acuña is a small Mexican border town near Del Rio, Texas. Day-tripping Americans come for shopping, cheap booze, and a shot at depravity in the compact tourist zone near the international bridge. Occasionally, a misguided traveler will think Acuña offers more than these predictable attractions and ask a taxi driver to show him "Real Mexico."

I was misguided when I ran into Diego. He was a short, strong-looking Mexican with a thick brown moustache and about 3 days stubble.

We agreed on a $20 tour of "everything to see in Acuña" and he pointed to a 1970-something Chevrolet that he swore was a taxi. The car was as scuffed and dirty as Diego's boots.

"Hey, Diego, when's the last time you washed this thing?" I asked.

"Hey, Amigo, when's the last time you try to keep a car clean in Acuña?"

"Why don't you fix that busted windshield, then?"

"If I change the window every time some rock come through it, I'm even more poor, My Friend."

All this made sense, so I got in and we bounced up the road for nearly a hundred yards before he stopped at an open-air foundry, and without so much as a "Wait here a second," or an "I'll be right back," he got out of the car. The lone welder shut off his torch and sat down with Diego on a wooden bench to smoke cigarettes.

Two or three cigarettes later, Diego got back in the car and said: "That Sumbitch still owe me a hundred bucks for that TV I get him."

"How'd you 'get' him a TV, Diego?" I asked, "You sure you're a taxi driver?"

"That Sumbitch still owe me a hundred bucks, Amigo. What else you need to know?"

A seriously upset Mexican taxi driver who can't see through his windshield is a tricky proposition, so two blocks up the road, when Diego suggested we stop for a beer, I agreed. Inside an unpainted concrete-block box decorated with pictures of naked women on last year's calendars and illuminated only by whatever light the doorway let in, Diego ordered two Tecates. After a few seconds silence, I knew it was my turn to buy.

Diego relaxed a little and said: "Last night, you know, my wife, she really piss me off. So I go out to drink beer and shoot pool. I drink beer all night. This morning I sleep an hour in the taxi. But now, I feel 'tenso.' You know…um…shaky."

Then he swallowed half his Tecate poured the rest in a plastic cup and said, "Let's go. I show you some more things." After a welding shop and a bar, what else could Diego show me?

In three minutes, I knew: "We got some big factories in Acuña. Wanna see?"

The "wanna see?" was clearly rhetorical because before I could say: "Why would I want to see a factory?" We were looking through a chain-link fence at a 300-foot-long windowless metal building and a couple of snarling scabby dogs that hoped we might be lunch.

"There!" Diego said, "Acuña got lots of big factories. I show you another one."

Before we found the next big factory, though, Diego started feeling a little tenso again, and he stopped at another concrete block building. It was bigger than the first one and it had electric lights and this year's naked women calendars. It also had pool tables, and Diego confessed that in this upscale place he had taken refuge from his wife.

Several guys were shooting 8 Ball for a lot more than fun and companionship. As Diego handed me a beer and waited for me to pay, he started shouting encouragement: "Fifty pesos you miss, you Sumbitch!"

Several hundred pesos later he suddenly remembered he had a taxi passenger somewhere in the bar and challenged me to a game: "You break, Amigo." I scratched on the break. Diego won. I bought two more beers, and we resumed the tour.

Diego was now much less tenso than when we'd left the welching welder. But even though he was feeling better, I was starting to have bigger concerns than just a smashed-in, mud-streaked windshield when he said: "I think you don't like factories, Amigo. Let's go someplace new."

I wasn't surprised when "someplace new" was another lightless concrete Tecate dispensary. But the new place did feature a jukebox repairman testing whether he could play mariachi music loud enough to shatter bricks. Otherwise, though, everything about the new place, right down to the "Gringo pays" rule, was just like the old places.

Before we settled into the music, Diego shouted something at me. There was no chance I could hear him, but when he picked up two plastic cups, I knew we were leaving.

About 90 seconds later, Diego fishtailed the Chevy to a stop in a cloud of dusty gravel, downed his beer in one noisy gulp and said: "You'll like this place. It's a Ladies Bar."

The Ladies Bar was the first place we'd been that really looked threatening. The bartender looked like a Lucha libre wrestler. Six drunk guys were arguing and pushing each other to emphasize major points of disagreement.

I was beginning to wonder what attraction this place could hold even for Diego when a sultry barefoot lady appeared at the side door, kicked a chicken out of the way and stepped into the bar. She put her arm around Diego. He kissed her and ordered three Tecates on the usual payment plan. Then Diego and his special friend moved to a corner table at the back of the bar and left me alone with the angry men.

Diego was starting to look pretty comfortable when one of the debaters got shoved hard to the floor and reached into his pocket. The bartender grabbed a baseball bat and leapt over the bar.

RIGHT THEN it was time for Diego to get the Gringo-Who-Hasn't-Paid-Me-Yet out of the Ladies Bar and into the taxi. A few minutes later we were standing on the street corner where fate first brought Diego and me together.

"You like my tour of Acuña?" he asked.

"It was special," I said, "Here's your money. I think I'll walk back to Del Rio."

"Oh no, Amigo. This is only twenty dollars. The price is twenty dollars AN HOUR! We been gone more than two hours. You owe me fifty bucks."

"Dammit, Diego," I said. "We spent nearly two hours in bars and I bought all the beers. You only showed me a factory fence and a welding shop. And I about got killed at that last place you took me. I know there's more to see here than that."

Diego looked pensive for a moment and then he said, "Sí, comprendo. Why you don't tell me you want to see a strip show? Let's get some tequila! We go right now!"

"Diego, I'll give you 25 dollars NOT to go to a strip show right now!" I said handing him the money.

He took it and said, "Thanks Amigo. Yeah, you right. Too early. We go tomorrow night."

Leaving Diego to look for his next victim, I ducked into Pancho's Regular Tourist Bar to work out my own case of tenso. An elderly American retiree was telling the bartender he was in Mexico "just killing time waiting to die."

"If he gets tired of waiting," I thought, "I've got just the man for him."

Chapter Twenty-Five
A Mexican Chinese New Year

Before coming to southern California, I lived as an expatriate "gweilo" (foreign devil) in Hong Kong for 20 years.

In Hong Kong, I had cultivated a taste for exotic south China cuisine like blood cake, goose web, and jellyfish. I had memorized a sequence of scathing Cantonese obscenities; but, except when I backed a losing horse at the Happy Valley Racetrack, I never mastered their correct use.

I also learned to appreciate the Chinese holidays: The Spring Festival with its lights and flowers, the Mid-Autumn Festival with its moon cakes and lantern parades. But most of all, I enjoyed Chinese New Year. The exchange of red "lai see" (lucky money) packets, the ubiquitous happiness and prosperity greeting of "Kung Hei Fat Choi," the magnificent fireworks over the harbor, and, of course, the five-day vacation became important annual rituals for me.

As Chinese New Year approached this year, I felt a tug of nostalgia for my old home, and I began to wonder if there was anywhere nearby that might allow me to indulge my enthusiasm for this wonderful holiday.

In that frame of mind, I ran across an entry in my Lonely Planet Guide to Baja California: "Today's Chinese population in Mexicali is around 2000, originating from Canton. It is the largest Chinese population in Mexico. The "Asociacion China de Mexicali...organizes cultural events, the big one being Chinese New Year."

"Great. Perfect," I thought, "two birds with one stone. I can practice my fledging Spanish and ring in the Lunar New Year in traditional style."

So, I took a tedious bus ride from San Diego via El Centro to dusty, windswept Calexico. I walked to the border and pushed through a revolving one-way metal gate into Mexicali.

I was looking for a street sign that would direct me to Avenida Juarez and the Chinese Association. I encountered two problems: First, most of the street signs were missing from their poles. Second, most of the few street markers that remained were bent in such a way as to direct you down the wrong street.

Luckily, Mexicali's Chinatown, or "La Chinesca" is close to the border crossing. Through a series of trial-and-error attempts I began to see a profusion of Chinese language signs and Chinese restaurants and cantinas.

My search was also aided by the guidebook's report that La Chinesca is a redlight district, and once you are in it, even in daytime, you would never mistake it for anything else. Eventually I found Av. Juarez and the offices of the Association.

The Association's office is only open a few hours a day on weekday mornings. Its exterior wall advertised a Mandarin language course and a few other cultural offerings, but I saw no evidence of preparation for the "big cultural event" of Chinese New Year.

I opened the building's gold ornamental gate and followed a dim corridor to small offices. A young woman of distant Chinese descent occupied the first office (unfortunately for her). She responded to my "buenas dias" in kind, but when I added "Kung Hei Fat Choi," she looked puzzled.

My Cantonese accent was always terrible, but surely, I thought, I couldn't get that simple phrase so wrong. She looked at me like she was watching a burro singing opera. Then with a sudden spark of recognition, like: "Oh! He's trying to speak Chinese!" she nodded.

My communication problems then began in earnest. I tried to explain in Spanish that I was interested in the Mexicali Fiesta of Chinese New Year. She said, "Que fiesta?" At this point because of vocabulary limitations, I began to pantomime "parade" and "fireworks" and "banquet," as I reverted to opera-singing burro status in her startled eyes.

Luckily, she was either patient or sympathetic enough to endure me long enough to grasp that I had lived in Hong Kong. Therefore, I much enjoyed the festivities of Chinese New Year and I wanted to witness them in Mexicali.

Then she explained the situation. No, there is no parade. No, there are no fireworks. Yes, there is a banquet, but for some reason, it is held three weeks after Chinese New Year Day. The banquet requires a ticket. It is for workers and officials of the Association and some Mexicali authority figures. Then she paused for a few seconds, as if trying to decide how to convey her final point tactfully, but she gave up and cut to the chase: "Pero, esta fiesta no es para usted!"

That sort of candor leaves little retort but a quick "muchas gracias por su tiempo, adios" while backing out the door and onto the streets of La Chinesca. I kept searching in vain for evidence that Chinese New Year was at hand. I saw no lion dancers or red posters of chubby children holding golden fruit.

I had given up when I spotted a sidewalk "tienda" apparently overflowing with red paper Chinese lanterns. Finally, I thought! But when I crossed the street and got closer, I discovered how much Tecate can-shaped piñatas resemble Chinese lanterns in the afternoon Mexican glare.

It was lunchtime. My quest had failed. I followed my guidebook's suggestion to the China Town Restaurant on Av. Madero. Inside, my holiday spirit was perked a little by a few festive decorations on the walls. I consoled myself with a couple of Tecates and a mound of Chop Suey Especial so grande that even a real burro could not have finished it.

When I finally admitted chop suey defeat, I received a fortune cookie that mistakenly informed me: "Eres un maestro de todos las situaticones." I paid an elderly Chinese lady at the register. I accepted my change and almost apologetically said, "Kung Hei Fat Choi."

She smiled, folded her hands together in the Chinese greeting and replied, "Kung Hei. Kung Hei. Gracias. Gracias."

It wasn't much of a Chinese New Year commemoration, but it would have to do for this misplaced "Master of all Situations."

I walked back to the "frontera" and joined a throng of hundreds waiting for permission to re-enter Calexico, and I thought, "Next year, Hong Kong."

Chapter Twenty-Six
Other People's Luggage

Imagine any Mr. and Mrs. Smith and their six-year-old daughter Suzie from Cairo, Illinois. They have just finished touring England on a bus. At Heathrow, they check in for their flight home. They give their bags to the counter agent, take their boarding passes and proceed to their departure gate where they board their on-time flight and return to the comforts of Middle America without incident.

Their bags are not so lucky. In an honest mistake, the counter agent directs their luggage not to the Corn Belt of America, but to the Capital of Egypt, where it festers in a storage room for long enough to change its legal status from "Lost" to "Unclaimed."

At this point, Mr. Smith's new sports jacket and slacks, his wife's best pants suit and sensible shoes and little Suzie's favorite stuffed bear and new coloring book, disappear through the unclaimed baggage wormhole and emerge along with the unclaimed baggage of other unfortunates from around the planet at a massive store on the edge of a small agreeable town in the hilly northeast corner of Alabama, USA. The store is named, appropriately, The Unclaimed Baggage Center. The town is Scottsboro.

The Unclaimed Baggage Center occupies a city block of floor space and has been selling the lost belongings of the world's unhappy air passengers since 1970. During that time, shoppers from every American state and more than 30 other countries have come to comb through the loot.

As you enter the Center from its abundant parking lot, you walk under a gazebo shaped archway embellished with the names of the world's popular travel destinations, like Cairo. Anyone who has ever entrusted their possessions to an airline, must, upon entering this shopping sanctum, feel a slight twinge of affinity for the former owners of the thousands of pieces of merchandise on sale. With more than a million items passing through the Center annually, it is a fair guess that most frequent flyers have contributed.

So many dispossessed travelers have asked if Center can help them find their things, the Center's website responds to this FAQ. The short answer is No. "By the time luggage reaches us, every effort has been made by the airline to find the rightful owners…This takes 3 to 4 months…Further, the volume of products coming through our store on a daily basis—much of it bought by shoppers within hours of reaching the sales floor would make it a virtual impossibility to track any one item."

Rough translation: Once your stuff gets here, it's not your stuff anymore. A couple of exceptions to this hard rule were a misplaced Space Shuttle camera, which was returned to NASA, and an overlooked F16 fighter jet guidance system, which was returned to the US military. I know…don't ask!

No matter how the goods arrive, the Center has well organized them for shoppers' convenience.

Among the most popular items at the Center are cameras. I don't know what happens to the snaps of the family at the beach, or the tree-line boulevard leading toward Notre Dame Cathedral, or Uncle Mack chugging that jug of Margaritas, but by the time the cameras go into the Center's display cabinets, those recorded memories are forever gone.

Near the cameras, lost eyewear is sold. In fact, so much lost eyewear is sold the section is divided between designer eyewear and ordinary eyewear. Why so many travelers would put their glasses in their checked luggage is one of the many imponderable questions the Center inspires.

Another important section near the eyewear and the cameras is devoted to sporting goods. Skiing equipment predominates and one seasoned shopper explained: "You can get some really good deals on skis here. These Alabama folks know everything there is to know about Nikons, but they don't know shit about snow skiing."

Jewelry is also extremely popular. In fact, the Center's web site reports finding a 41-carat emerald and a 5.8-carat diamond ring in lost bags. But even the less illustrious jewelry is pretty stunning. The array of gold bracelets and necklaces, gemstones and watches could be found in top rate jewelry stores. The shoppers at this counter show a different level of sophistication than the ones sorting through other people's underwear in the next room.

From scouring the items like jewelry, cameras and eyeglasses, which had no business being checked in the first place, the bargain hunters can move into the much larger, clothing sections. Every conceivable item of formal, casual, sporty and intimate apparel is arranged by size. Women can browse for cocktail dresses, business suits, blouses, skirts, sportswear, or lingerie. Men can buy tuxedoes, sports coats, athletic nylon or motorcycle leather jackets, socks, ties, or a pair of Jockey briefs the size of a spinnaker at a rock bottom price.

Between the ladies and men's clothing section is the Center's Art Department. A nearby sign reports that one unrecognized art treasure was sold for $50, but the lucky buyer later discovered it was worth more than $10,000. That picture may not, however, have much resembled the Tijuana black felt portraits I thumbed through looking for my own personal fortune.

Before the happy but harried shoppers line up at the cash registers, they are encouraged to visit the small alcove which forms the Center's museum of Astounding Unclaimed Baggage. A violin made and signed by a student of Stradivarius, a 3500-year-old Egyptian artifact, an original Jim Hensen life-sized puppet, all found their way here. The thoughtful shopper who visits this exhibit and who is not still worried about whether to take the red or the black secondhand bra may possibly ask: "How could anyone lose something that valuable?" And then ask: "How is it possible that after at least 90 days of intensive tracking by the airline, that the rightful owners of these extraordinary items could not be found?"

The Center provokes many such thoughts. Even in the midst of the shopping frenzy, it would be the very hardened bargain hunter who was not a little saddened by some of the personal losses on display. The most obvious are in the children's sections. A favorite doll or stuffed animal dragged lovingly around on a family vacation has vanished into oblivion. A bedtime storybook, ritually reread so often the exhausted Mom recites it in her own sleep, is just gone.

But even if a shopper overlooks the small sorrow of a child's tiny loss, almost everyone who has sufficient consciousness not to buy someone else's Jockey briefs will pause a moment in front of the lost wedding dress display. Did the bride lose it on her way to the wedding? When the baggage carousel finally stopped turning and the last piece of luggage was trolleyed off, was she standing there alone? Did the luggage agent tell her not to worry? Did he assure her it would arrive on the next plane? Did he tell her: "Worst case, Honey, it'll be here tomorrow, never you mind?"

But it wasn't there on the next plane, and it wasn't there tomorrow. And as any visitor to The Unclaimed Baggage Center could have told her, the "worst case" is very much worse than that.

Chapter Twenty-Seven
One Night in the French Quarter

Just past midnight, Pat O'Brien's famous New Orleans French Quarter bar dropped the price of Dixie Beer to two for one. I handed the bartender a few dollars and collected two Dixies. Right then, a chestnut-haired girl in a Tulane University T-shirt stepped up to the bar and ordered something expensive and foreign. With some rebuke about Louisiana loyalty, I offered her my other Dixie. She took my beer, cancelled her order, and that is how I met Stephanie.

We told each other that the people we'd come with had already gone home, but we didn't know them well, anyway. And then we said whatever you say to someone you have just met when you're afraid they will leave if the conversation dies.

Eventually the beer prices went up, or my money ran out, or we just decided we needed oxygen, and we went outside. On Chartres Street, we bumped into three French seamen. Inexplicably, these sailors imagined their mother tongue might be a useful aid to conversation in the French Quarter. A couple of Oklahoma tourists were proving them seriously wrong when Stephanie turned up.

Stephanie was either born speaking French, or she had breathed the language in whole as a child. She spoke French so beautifully, that as soon as I heard her, I knew those sailors would follow us wherever we went. We wandered all over the Quarter with Stephanie explaining the sights to them, and with me vainly trying to construct a French sentence that didn't contain the word: *merde*.

Inevitably, we came into Café du Monde for caffeine and chicory at three in the morning. And there and then, in one of those transcendental intersections of space and time that reaffirm the existence of God, three French girls appeared at our table, sat down with the sailors, and dismissed Stephanie and me from further tour guide duties.

"Let's go dancing," Stephanie said, in the first English words I had heard in hours. She led me down a dark alley to an unmarked door. Without so much as a knock, or a "Joe sent me," she opened the door and admitted me to a pre-dawn club where a zydeco band was playing, liquor was free, and dance floor mobility was severely restricted.

For years after that, whenever I visited New Orleans, I desperately tried and failed to find that door again. I might as well have been seeking the Grail. It was like I had just imagined it.

Whether that party ever ended, or we left early, or I really had only imagined it, I am no longer certain. But I will always be certain of the shrill whistle of a locomotive engine chugging up the Mississippi River levee tracks toward the old Jax Brewery, and the train's crew cheering Stephanie and me as we stood on the riverbank watching the sun rise. The moment was shattered, but it was nice to be appreciated by so many enthusiastic strangers.

There was nothing left to do but acknowledge their cheers, find the Tulane T-shirt, and trudge off through the scattered refuse and colliding odors of a French Quarter Saturday dawn. At my hotel, we just said goodbye. And then the French-speaking Louisiana girl who knew where the door was, disappeared up St. Charles Avenue.

Hong Kong, Taiwan, Macau

Chapter Twenty-Eight
Another Hong Kong Afternoon

A Chinese Gollum squatting on a concrete stool
Savors a second-hand cigarette butt
And searches the sacred text of his racing form
For a path to redemption.

At a nearby meat shop a man in a blood-stained shirt
Mashes rice and grease into a Styrofoam bucket
With his wet bare hand.

A small bent woman with a broken flip-flop
Mines the rubbish cylinder for lunch
And aluminum cans.

The Pussy Cat Club illuminates its offer
Of young girls at cheap prices
As the first shift of high-heeled workers
Trudges upstairs.

An abandoned hand trolley
Piled with cardboard and garbage
Blocks the path to a fruit stand.

A legless beggar interrupts his kowtows
To re-count the contents of his cup
But still finds only four coins.

Slumped against the Seven Eleven
An incongruous Caucasian in a rugby shirt
Ignores a rat and cradles
A quart of Tsingtao in his lap.

A jaded whore-hawker in front of a topless bar
Lights joss sticks on the sidewalk
And summons old men to Happy Hour.

And when I finish this Tsingtao
I think I'll get up and go there
For some of that half-priced beer.

Chapter Twenty-Nine
Place Your Bets
The History and Mythology of Hong Kong Horse Racing

It's drizzling rain and I'm standing here at Hong Kong's Happy Valley racetrack marking a betting ticket. The marks represent nine horses in a three-way parlay called the "Triple Trio." The ticket costs US$1.30 (HK$10). If the picks are right, it's worth US$32 million. Just pick the first three horses in any order in each of the third, fourth and sixth races. How hard can that be? Don't ask the players who bet more than $15 million the previous week. No winners. Those bets carry over and you add a similar amount from this week's betting, and you have one riveted city.

Triple Trio (or 3T) is the mantra of Hong Kong's gamblers these days. It is the central god of a city that worships at the betting altar. Everyone is a believer. In fact, "Have you bought your 3T?" has replaced "Have you eaten lunch?" as the daily afternoon greeting in this city that really likes to eat lunch. But what it likes even more is getting rich. And winning the Triple Trio is the express train to Easy Street.

Never mind the odds. It's not about luck or skill. It's about summoning divine intervention. This is the place where dragons inhabit mountains and burning paper appeases ancestral spirits. Nothing is left purely to chance. You try to pick the best horses, but you also throw in a few auspicious numbers for insurance. If it is a rainy day, you also add the gray horses. And don't forget the old horses because, "They know the way." If all of this paranormal analysis goes on for a plain old 2-1 win bet, imagine what goes on for a 25 million to 1 Triple Trio.

The Jockey Club introduced the Triple Trio wager in 1997, perhaps to distract the public from the impending handover of Hong Kong to mainland China. Whatever their reason, Triple Trio was a clever revenue enhancement for an organization that handled over 17 billion US dollars in racing bets in 2021.

To see how far horse racing has come here, it helps to look where it started—in a soggy rice paddy during the heyday of European imperial expansion. The history of Hong Kong racing and in many ways, the early development of Hong Kong itself, is tied to the history of that old paddy field.

In 1841, the British Royal Navy landed on Hong Kong to take possession of the island during the First Opium War. After they hoisted the Union Jack, raised a rum to their young Queen, and consecrated a plot of ground for the Church of England, they got down to the serious business of finding a place to race horses. The site they picked—on land between the harbor and the island's central mountain range and beside the colony's first cemetery—became known in English as Happy Valley. The Chinese name is more to the point: Pau Ma Dei means "running horse field." Nearly 180 years later, the course is still there.

The valley itself in the mid-19th century was flat and swampy. The villagers of nearby Wong Nei Chung (yellow mud stream) used it for rice farming and other messy activities. Before the discovery of quinine, it was a death trap. Ancient markers in the cemetery stand in solemn testament to the ravages of malaria there. Driven away by "the Fever," early colonists settled the sea front and hills further west in what are now the districts of Central and Sheung Wan.

By 1845, the settlers had drained Happy Valley and dug a channel, or nullah, to carry the water runoff and other drainage from the mountain and village into the harbor. It then became possible to race horses at what is now arguably the most famous track in Asia,

In early photos taken from the grandstand area, the harbor is clearly visible. But after decades of land reclamation, the tight-bunched, high-rise, fume-hazed urban muddle of Causeway Bay now borders Happy Valley. From the rail in front of the grandstand today, not only can you not see the harbor, but you also have to crane your neck to see the sky.

Because of the island's shortage of flat land, recreational use of Happy Valley's infield grounds has also reflected the city's evolving interests. In the beginning, the marshy infield was used by foreigners for shooting water birds. This activity would evoke no enthusiasm today from the towers of apartment dwellers packed along the back straight. Now a patchwork of soccer, field hockey, and rugby grounds crisscross the infield. On weekends, when it's not being used for concerts, the place is a massive sports carnival.

Happy Valley's 9-storey grandstand holds up to 40,000 punters. A century and a half ago, at the spot of today's grandstand, "matsheds" of woven rattan and bamboo sheltered well-off Chinese while a small three storey wooden pavilion accommodated the colonials. Alongside the rail ran the noxious nullah, which from contemporary descriptions, may more have resembled an open sewer than a canal. A large boulder, which still sits at the end of the back straight served as a favorite vantage point for Chinese who didn't get into the matsheds.

Race meetings at Happy Valley remain a microcosm of Hong Kong society. Jockey Club members and their guests now go through guarded turnstiles up elevators to plush boxes with private betting windows. Less affluent Chinese, Indians, Filipinos, and expatriate Europeans stand on the pavement next to the track where they munch chicken legs, slurp noodles, and drink cheap beer. Not much intermingling happens down there unless someone's beer gets kicked over while he is trying to balance a bowl of noodles in one hand and mark his betting card with the other. Traditional Cantonese and English expletives are usually then exchanged, which in translation, are remarkably similar.

As a practical matter, whether in the boxes or at the rail, the best way to watch the races is on the enormous television screen in the middle of the infield. Almost everyone at the track, except the ones queuing up to buy more beer can see it. The screen also means that you don't actually need horses to be "at the races." On days when the races are held at Hong Kong's other track across the harbor in Shatin, the Happy Valley track still fills up with gamblers who bet on races broadcast on the big screen. The experience is virtually the same, even down to fans jostling to the rail as the starting bell sounds to get a better view of horses that aren't there.

I sometimes go to the races even when there are no horses around. Today there is an international cup race as well as the $32 million Triple Trio running at Shatin. Clutching their 3T tickets, the Happy Valley fans' excitement builds as the horses settle in at a starting post 10 miles away. The great screen shows us the last horse is in. His "mafoo" secures the gate and ducks out of harm's way. We jostle to the rail. The racing god will surely descend and one of us will at last be free...Aaaand they're off!!!

The fact that I finished writing this is certain evidence that my 3T ticket was just another bit of useless cardboard. But someone near me did win and in that moment after he sank to his knees with his winning ticket, he knew there really is a racing god. He later learned that this god has a sense of humor: 38 other winners were sharing his prize.

Chapter Thirty
Hong Kong: The Number One Wanchai Rule

[Wanchai is a diverse entertainment district. Originally popular with British and American sailors on shore leave, it now accommodates expatriates and visitors of all nationalities]

A female undercover cop in Neptune, the notorious subterranean disco in Wanchai's red light district, pulled out her badge and shouted over the band at my well-served friend. "Excuse me, Sir. Did you just say: 'You like my ass?'"

"Umm…No officer. No! I said, 'I'd like to take you to Mass.'"

"I see. You watch yourself," she warned and turned away.

It was a great recovery, but Chris had forgotten The Number One Wanchai Rule, so I reminded him: "Never, never chat up Hong Kong girls in Neptune." They are always cops. The Thai girls, the Filipinas, the Russians are there for the music or the money, but the Hong Kong girls are there for law enforcement.

"Yeah, I know," Chris said, "I should have it written on my arm."

"You should have it tattooed on your…."

I didn't get to finish the thought. Just then, all the lights in Neptune switched to high beam and the Filipino cover band jolted to a halt halfway through the guitar solo of Lynard Skynard's "Free Bird." While everyone was blinking into the glare and recoiling from a clear look at the stranger they'd been drinking with, the entire Wanchai police force charged down the stairs and half the "customers," who'd previously just been standing around, held up badges.

Enough cops to round up every man, woman and Wookie in the Neptune fanned out across the bar and dance floor. For the Lithuanian showgirl with the expired tourist visa sipping my drink, it was time to panic, or at least it was time to drink up.

Welcome to Friday night at Neptune. Bring your ID. Prepare to stay a while. The bar stays open, but you can't leave. Hang out, have another San Mig and watch the funny people. Watch, for instance, the famous Australian expat executive at the bar turn green.

"What's this about?" he whispered to his pal.

"Just a routine immigration check, mate. No dramas, just show 'em your ID and they go on to the next bloke."

"But I don't have my ID with me!"

"Well, that could be a spot of bother, especially if there's paparazzi about. Tell ya what, just flash 'em your knighthood medal and tell 'em you're Sir Mick Jagger."

It might have worked, but the idea was never tested. Before they reached us, the police achieved their arrest quota. A few Southeast Asian females without papers and one gweilo man who had clearly forgotten The Number One Wanchai Rule were frog marched up the stairs and into the waiting vans to the murmured relief of the remaining crowd.

To signal the end of the excitement, the lights re-dimmed and the guitarist struck the next chord of "Free Bird." The famous executive slumped onto the bar and everywhere the eternal dialogue resumed: "What your name? Where you from? You buy me drink? You take me out? How much? How much? How much?"

I turned to Chris and offered to buy the next round, but remarkably, he declined. His near-miss ordeal seemed to have brought him to a certain epiphany. He set down a full San Miguel and quietly announced that he would rather go next door to Delaney's Irish Pub and watch cricket re-runs, alone. He said he thought he needed to leave Neptune out of his life for a long time and then he stood up and walked off.

But as the guitarist reached the final crescendo and the dance floor erupted, I saw Chris look over his shoulder. And I knew he'd be back before I finished my beer.

Chapter Thirty-One
Remembering The Cold War In Kinmen, Taiwan

A convenient weekend break from the noise and bustle of Taipei is a one-hour flight to the island of Kinmen. Although Kinmen is controlled by Taiwan, it lies only eight kilometers from the Chinese Mainland coast, within sight of Xiamen.

These days, about the only way to get shelled on Kinmen is to overdose on the local sorghum-based 116 proof Kaoliang liquor. But, for thirty years, from 1949 to 1979, the possibility of being actually shelled by Chinese artillery was almost as life threatening as too much Kaoliang liquor.

Looking around the sleepy backwater of Kinmen now, it is hard to believe it was nearly the catalyst to global nuclear war in the 1950's, when it was more commonly known as Quemoy. The trouble began when the Chinese Nationalist army fleeing the Communists from the mainland dug in for a last stand on Kinmen's beaches. In a dramatic reversal of their fortunes, the Nationalists repelled advancing Communist armies and Kinmen became a remote outpost of what the West then called "Free China."

The United States signed a defence treaty with Taiwan in 1954 and the Communists punished Kinmen with sustained artillery shelling. About the same time, Chiang Kai-shek built up troop strength on the 150 sq. km. island to around 100,000 men while he planned his quixotic quest to recover the Motherland. Finally, by August 1958, Mao had enough of the offshore mosquito and launched a massive bombardment, which lasted nearly two months and killed hundreds of soldiers and civilians.

The Cold War's two major antagonists, the US and the USSR, then walked onto Kinmen's stage. The US Secretary of State, John Foster Dulles, threatened to drop nuclear weapons on China if they attempted to invade and the US Seventh Fleet sailed into the Taiwan Straits. Mao, looking for an equalizer, tried to enlist Khrushchev to counter-nuke America. Luckily for the future of Mankind, Khrushchev declined. Tensions eased, and "Quemoy" forever entered the lexicon of the Cold War.

From 1958 until 1979, a bizarre accommodation occurred: The Communists would fire artillery at Kinmen on even numbered days of the month and the Nationalists would counter-fire on the odd numbered days of the month. My Kinmen driver was a young girl then and remembered being herded into the family shelter whenever the shelling started. She recalled once, when the first explosions began especially late, telling her grandmother that she didn't want to hide anymore she just wanted to sleep. "You'll sleep forever then!" her grandmother shouted, as she jerked the reluctant child into her shelter.

Now, Kinmen is a pleasant, agricultural island covered in fields of maize, sorghum, peanuts and taro, and dotted by small temples. Its principal tourist attractions fall into two main categories: South China clan villages caught in a Qing Dynasty time warp and decaying Cold War defence relics.

In Kinmen, all villages post a granite statue of a "Wind Lion" at their northwest corner to protect against the ravages of the monsoon. Wind Lions, standing upright and usually wearing a red cape, have thankfully replaced soldiers as the prominent symbol of Kinmen.

The best Wind Lion stands outside the village of Qionglin. If a visitor to Kinmen had time to visit only one traditional village, Qionglin should be it. When I went there, dozens of women sat in front of their houses shucking oysters. Qionglin's complex maze of alleys and warrens was presumably laid out to confound enemies and tourists. It succeeded on me. After half an hour of aimlessly searching for Kinmen's most photographed Wind Lion, I gave up and asked one of the oyster ladies for directions.

"It's at the temple, of course! Where else would it be?" was her helpful response. Actually, it wasn't that helpful because I was also still looking for the temple. When I at last accidentally stumbled onto the temple, I still couldn't locate the Wind Lion. Reluctantly, I approached a second oyster lady and learned, "It's behind the temple, of course! Where else would it be?"

My quest was rewarded by a ten-foot tall fierce-visaged red-caped granite lion standing on his hind legs, facing down acres of swaying sorghum and daring a monsoon to annoy his village. As an extra bonus, just beyond the Wind Lion, is the exit of a military tunnel where, not so long ago, Nationalist armies ducked Communist artillery and planned their next moves in the great Chinese chess game.

Once you've finished your clan village and wind lion tour, it is time to take on the military history. Kinmen is still quite evidently a front line. Soldiers are everywhere. If they are now one-tenth their former strength, spotting a civilian must have been difficult in the past.

Kinmen is a Swiss cheese of military tunnels. Many tunnels are now open to the public. Some are much more pleasant than others. The tunnel that ends by the Qionglin Wind Lion, for example, is narrow, dark and ankle deep in water for most of its 250-meter length. By the time you pop out, your shoes are sloshing but you are relieved to breathe free again.

Armies needed five years to dig most tunnels with hand-held jackhammers. Some provided vital shelter for gunboats during the regular bombardments. The best tunnel for tourists is on Lieyu, a tiny island a few hundred meters west of Kinmen proper. Also hand-hewn from granite, Siwei Tunnel sheltered front-line troops who survived the sea crossing from Kinmen as they made their way from the landing pier to the dangerous battle stations closest to the Chinese guns.

Another interesting feature of Lieyu is the island's circumferential road. It is exactly the width of a 1960's vintage Chinese tank. Both edges of the road are paved in hard rubber to facilitate tank mobility for the home team. The centerline of the road is cobbled to facilitate laying anti-tank mines to greet any visitors who might make it across the strait. Today, cars generally try to drive between the rubber and the cobbles making for some anxious moments rounding bends at speed.

Kinmen abounds in military museums and shrines. The Kouningtou War Museum, just behind the northwestern beaches, explains that, in a Normandy style invasion, Communist soldiers, ferried in fishing junks, were overwhelmingly defeated in 1949. This museum contains several well-executed oil paintings of battle scenes with hour-by-hour explanations of the hostilities.

As inspiring as the paintings are, however, the best way to get the real feel for the battle is to go to the actual landing beach. I asked the museum information desk how to get to the beach, but was rebuked: "Why would you want to go there? It looks just like the picture."

Maybe so, but I asked my driver to take me to the most accessible section of the war beach, Lung Kou. She too was baffled. "Why go there? The nicest beaches are in the south. Lung Kou is no good for swimming. And they haven't found all the mines yet." But persistence paid off and she took me to Taiwan's own Omaha Beach.

Lung Kuo is a long curve of white sand defended by rows of concrete-implanted two-meter-long iron spikes pointed at China. Behind the spikes, abandoned bunkers, positioned to spray machine gun fire across the water, now sprout huge cactus plants. Weaving through the remaining mines, strong, old, black-dressed women harvest oysters from the rusted spikes and concrete encasements under the watchful eyes of well-armed soldiers.

After this beach tour, retire to Kinmen's only town, Jincheng. Jincheng's shops offer locally made products like a peanut candy, called gongtang, ceramics, bottles of fiery Kaoliang liquor, and choppers and knives hammered from artillery shells. A few street-side cooks fry up local delicacies like sweet potato, taro, and oyster buns.

A restaurant called The Red Chamber entices tourists to sample Kaoliang liquor by mixing it into exotic fruit cocktails. The evening I visited, my waitress was explaining the comparative virtues of Kaoliang with mango and iced tea, with orange and passion fruit, with tomato juice and lime, when she was interrupted by a wizened old fellow who said: "Forget all that! If you're not drinking Kaoliang straight," (which to me would be like drinking gasoline straight), "then drink it like this." At which he mixed a 50-50 glass of warm Taiwan Beer and Kaoliang and downed it in one gulp with no obvious effect.

If you can take thirty years of artillery shelling, you can take anything. Not so seasoned, I politely declined.

Chapter Thirty-Two
Thirsting For Knowledge

A Visit to the Macau Wine Museum

In the former Portuguese colony of Macau, the Tourist Office pamphlet promoting the wine museum offered an incredible enticement. Admission with wine tasting costs 15 Macau patacas, (US$2) and "of the new wines, about fifty of them are available for tasting." The pamphlet further promised the "wines were presented in an appealing way which allows the imagination to go through atmospheres," as an imagination would after tasting 50 wines.

It sounded like an incredible offer, so I fronted up at the ticket office. Here I learned the sobering truth.

"Yes, there are over 50 wines for tasting, but only six are available each day. No, the 15 pataca ticket doesn't buy the storeroom, it is only good for one drink." Still, 15 patacas is a pretty good price for a glass of decent Madeira, so I bought six tickets.

After passing through a screening device, which deters visitors from removing the 80-year-old vintage ports from the salesroom, I was in the museum. The first exhibit was a long wooden oxcart loaded with an enormous wicker basket full of plastic grapes. Where the ox should have been, a thin wooden stake precariously propped up this heavy vehicle and its burden of plastic grapes. A sign prohibited sitting, squatting, or leaning on the cart.

As interesting as that was, it wasn't what I'd come for. The wine dispensary was a small table near the entrance overseen by a helpful sommelier. "We have white wine, red wine, white port, red port, brandy and Madeira," she explained. "Where is your ticket and what do you want?" "Madeira, thank you," I said, "I'm going for alcohol content."

Thus armed, I walked into the museum's first gallery, which is decorated in the style of a Portuguese taverna with long wooden tables and benches. Along the walls are exhibits of all the wine producing regions of Portugal. For each region there is a map, a description of the grapes grown there, a rack of local wines, and a male and female mannequin dressed in the region's traditional costumes.

A Mainland Chinese tour group monopolized the tables, so I gravitated toward the Dao region exhibit because its mannequins had the coolest costumes. The guy wore a full-body suit of straw from hat to shoes. After a couple of glasses, I tried to engage him in a duet of "If I Only Had a Brain," but I couldn't. Eventually I had to sing it alone.

From that exhibit, I learned the Dao region of north central Portugal produces "Bastardo Tinto" grapes and it has been making wine out of those little bastards since the 8th century. I also learned that grape farmers worry about things called peduncles, pedials and bunch shape.

Peduncles come in short, average and long. Pedials can be short or long with loose or clinging fruit.

Intriguingly, the bunch shape of the "Alvarinho" is small, hanging double and fairly compact. But pathetically, the "Redondo Reguengos Vidigueira" is very small, yellowish green with a soft colorless pulp.

Beyond the wine exhibition room, is a faux wine cellar with an authentic musty smell. Here, the museum displays the various implements used in viniculture from copper serpentine fermentation tanks, to wooden barrels, to earthen jars, to wooden grape-stomping vats full of plastic grapes.

You can get through that part pretty quickly and go to the museum's collection of really expensive dusty bottles of ancient wine. This display, which includes a Madeira bottled in the year of Waterloo, is protected by industrial-strength chains and padlocks.

I was just finishing my tour, which is to say, I was just finishing my sixth glass of Madeira. On my way out, I was walking past a photo exhibit of modern Portuguese wine production, when suddenly I heard a loud thud that could only be an enormous wicker basket full of plastic grapes crashing off a fallen wooden oxcart. Then I heard the rapid stomping of twelve leather boots that could only be six security guards rushing to secure the plastic grapes, followed by a chorus of five Cantonese words suggesting maternal incest.

A breakfast wine tour group had apparently violated the No-Sitting-On-The-Oxcart rule with predictable consequences and the ensuing chaos consumed the previously placid museum. The guards were shouting and shoving and pointing at the "No Sitting" sign. The tour group, whose members were the only eyewitnesses to the incident, seemed to be offering the explanation of supernatural intervention and oxcart levitation. An angry crowd was building, and most troubling, the sommelier had backed away from her duties.

Things were getting ugly fast when a quick-thinking elderly Portuguese gentleman stepped up to the guards and explained that as a child in the old country, he had indeed heard stories of levitating oxcarts. So, perhaps, if everyone just calmed down and picked up the plastic grapes, we could all get some more wine.

It worked. Order was restored. The tour group left. The sommelier returned. I bought another ticket and allowed my imagination to go through another atmosphere.

If I only had a brain.

Chapter Thirty-Three
The 2003 Sars Epidemic in Hong Kong (Three Parts)

[During the early days of 2003 a mysterious highly infectious deadly respiratory disease appeared in Southern China and quickly spread to Hong Kong. It was eventually named Severe Acute Respiratory Syndrome, or SARS.

Like Covid 19, SARS was a coronavirus. Unlike Covid 19, it did not become a pandemic, and it was basically finished as an epidemic within half a year. But, at the beginning, no one knew what was coming and most of us were frightened. By the end, all of us were exhausted and relieved.

The following three articles were written for an American newspaper as Hong Kong responded to the progression of the SARS epidemic.]

Part One
SARS: the Beginning

The shelves of instant noodles, Chinese vegetables, chicken, and pork at my local grocery in central Hong Kong are almost bare today. Rice is a distant memory. It was all wiped out in minutes, not hours, by swarming panic buying launched by a hoax.

An April Fool's Day Web site announced that because of the escalating atypical pneumonia crisis, the World Health Organization had declared Hong Kong an "infected port." No one gets in. No one gets out.

Although this status is normally reserved for massive plague and cholera outbreaks, it was an extremely plausible rumor here because this mysterious and sometimes fatal virus has been doubling its tally of victims every few days.

I don't know how many people actually saw the fake report, but in this edgy city that hates to miss a meal, the word spread instantly and with the predictable response: "Get food!"

The government quickly dispelled the rumor with TV broadcasts and text messages to every cell phone user. It all came too late to save the rice and noodles, but luckily for Western residents, the corn flakes, gin and hamburger meat were largely unscathed.

Hong Kong feels like a siege town this week. Virtually everyone wears a mask. Many wear gloves to touch public areas such as elevator buttons and escalator handrails. Radio ads feature a sneezer being shouted down by an angry mob for not covering his face.

Cleaning, mopping, spraying are incessant. Signs in English and Chinese sprang up everywhere admonishing personal hygiene in this place where serial spitting was once a national competitive event.

More than 700 have been infected in a few weeks here. At the time of this writing, 16 had died. Last Monday, an entire 30-story apartment block was sealed off and all the residents who hadn't already fled were quarantined because one person managed to infect nearly 300 people there in a matter of days.

Bad news increases as rapidly as the number of victims. Schools for 1 million students were closed and public events were cancelled. Airlines were trying to contact passengers from three flights between Hong Kong and China that had carried infected passengers.

Continual TV footage from the quarantined apartment block showed scenes of taped-off corridors and crowds of fully masked and gowned police and medical staff moving into the lobby.

Last Wednesday, the U.S. Consulate announced the voluntary evacuation of non-essential staff and families and several countries imposed restrictions on passengers arriving from here. And finally on Wednesday night, the World Health Organization basically advised: "Don't go to Hong Kong, for the love of God."

But here we are. Masked-up, hunkered-down, practicing personal hygiene and wondering: What next? Leaving is still possible, but it may be riskier than staying. The only land route out leads through the mother of all infected areas, Guangdong, China, and it appears that flying may be one of the best ways to get sick.

The potential for disaster is obvious if you look at the environment and the recent pattern of infection. It is clearly established that the virus spreads rapidly through close personal contact and if Hong Kong is anything, it is a city of close personal contact. Nearly all of its 7 million people live in high-rise congestion, like the quarantined building.

Walking down a sidewalk at rush hour or lunchtime resembles a pedestrian version of bumper cars. Busy local food stalls jam as many complete strangers as humanly possible around small tables.

Most people live a long way from work and those who can't afford cars or taxis squeeze into public transportation with only internal ventilation systems.

Whether this volatile mix will lead to a pandemic or the drastic changes in hygiene habits and the government's actions will see us through is still an open question. The outcome may still be very far in the future.

But the heroes of the story are now and will continue to be the local medical community. Hong Kong doctors and nurses fight on despite incredible personal exposure. Some have died. Many are ill.

Their e-mails of encouragement to each other often reach the general public. "Inevitably we will all become infected eventually," one said. "The ultimate protection against this new virus is our immunity. Follow all precautions. Take care, buddy."

Good advice.

Chapter Thirty-Four

Part Two
SARS: Turning the Corner

Little by little, Hong Kong people are starting to emerge from their holes. Blinking into the stark sunlight, they are gradually removing their facemasks, freeing themselves of the recycled garlic they have been breathing for months. I knew things were improving when my paralegal, who has been telecommuting from an offshore island for five weeks came back to the office today decidedly relaxed and sporting what looked suspiciously like a five-week suntan.

New cases have been in single digits all week. Yesterday's four was a record low. Today only five. It's too soon to dance in the streets, of course, with mainland China's cases still peaking and 300,000 daily land border crossings, but even the World Health Organization, which awarded us pariah status in early April, seems encouraged. They have proclaimed we will become; I think the technical term is, "A Regular Place," if we have three consecutive days at or below 5 new cases.

World-wide TV images of our masked population have obviously exacerbated the economic downturn caused by the disease itself. Now that things are looking up, local business leaders' opinions are mixed as to whether masks should still be worn. The president of the American Chamber of Commerce said caution should be taken and urged people to follow the Health Department's advice, while his British counterpart basically said the equivalent of: "Take the bloody things off, for Christ's sake!"

Some people may be sorry to see the masks go. For instance, they gave deniability to being seen at the wrong place or with the wrong person. But for many, they inhibited intimacy. Karaoke bars, which often double as hostess clubs, are on the government's list of industries that need to be rescued from the SARS downturn. And massage parlours are shuttered; business was rubbed out.

The masks can also cause some difficult personal choices. Do I cut a hole in my mask for a beer straw? The Surgeon General advises against it, but if you don't, the mask gets soggy. Can I inhale this cigar through it? You can, but you need the special flameproof type, especially if you have a beard.

Some professions have been especially hard hit by SARS. For instance, that scrawny fellow who wants to give you a hand towel in the lavatory gets very few takers today. On the other hand, some businesses have experienced a boom time. The previously unknown endeavour of lift button/doorknob wiper blossomed overnight. People who haven't worked in years have been handed mops and marshalled onto the pavements. And SARS has done for Clorox what AIDS did for Durex.

When we are finally out of the woods, there will obviously be some nostalgia. I'll always remember that Chinese lady carrying her masked miniature poodle down my street; and that paperboy lifting his mask to spit on the sidewalk in the traditional Hong Kong style; and that hiker near the top of a steep mountain, blue-faced and bent-over, gasping through his face mask. These views were especially poignant. And for group fun, the food riots set off by the April Fool's Day internet hoax were memorable, too.

The media have been desperately trying to boost morale with mixed results. The local paper held an email SARS haiku contest. The overwhelming response caused them to end the contest three days early with the headline "No More Haikus!" Entrants thoroughly explored the mask and hygiene culture. "That almond-eyed girl/Looks sexy in her tight top/And matching blue mask," was one of my contributions to this important new branch of literature.

The same paper also sponsored a campaign to collect money to buy protective equipment for front line health care workers, which netted millions of dollars. But occasionally it lost its way, like when it ran a photo of hordes of shoppers blithely walking past a legless beggar with an empty cup lying face down on a rain-drenched sidewalk, with the caption, "Hong Kong is returning to normalcy." If Pulitzers were awarded for irony, no one else need apply.

The government is also a contender for irony awards. Just before SARS really got up to speed, they commissioned a tourism promotion ad, which featured the song "Take My Breath Away." It was still running in Australia as the death toll was climbing.

But enough criticism of a government and a population that have done an extraordinary job of getting us to where we are today. If we have one more day of five or fewer new cases, the masks are coming off. The last question is what's the best way to celebrate? Today someone thoughtfully suggested burning a million facemasks. Since air pollution will kill more people here than SARS this year, who could disagree?

Part Three
SARS: The End of the Emergency

DATELINE HONG KONG MAY 25, 2003

HONG KONG SARS EMERGENCY ENDING.
TWENTY DAY AVERAGE FIVE NEW CASES.
QUARANTINES THROUGHOUT CITY LIFTED.
W.H.O: "HONG KONG NOW REGULAR CITY."
GOVERNMENT LUMINARIES CLAIM CREDIT.
UNMASKED REVELERS JAM STREETS.
DRINKS 2 FOR 1 ALL NIGHT EVERYWHERE.
FRENCH BEAUTY WHIPS OFF HER SHIRT.
FLINGS IT INTO THE JUBILENT CROWD.
HONG KONG IS BACK.

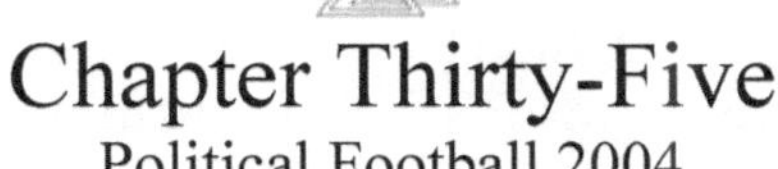

Chapter Thirty-Five
Political Football 2004

I began what was supposed to be a two-year expatriate assignment in Hong Kong in May 1985. But, perhaps, even more important in local history, May 1985 was the last time Hong Kong played China in a Soccer World Cup qualifying match. That match resulted in a 2-1 Hong Kong victory which eliminated China from the 1986 World Cup Finals and ignited a major riot in Beijing. Last month, they played again.

I remember having second thoughts about my new career path as I watched those riots on television 19 years ago. But before I could call the airline for a return ticket, several Old China Hands reassured me that it was just an ordinary soccer mob, and rather a benign one at that, compared to Liverpool at the time. If it had been a political riot, they explained, the home side would have brought tanks as well as rocks and clubs. I resolved to hang around, and now, near the end of that no longer new career, I was ready for the rematch.

China-Hong Kong could never be "just a soccer match." Like USA-USSR ice hockey during the Cold War; England-Argentina soccer after the Falklands; and India-Pakistan in any sport at any time, politics is also in play.

Nineteen years ago, the China-Hong Kong match was played shortly after the conclusion of the initial agreements between Britain and China on the Hong Kong handover. China was in a triumphant mood. After 150 years of British occupation, which had outrageously resulted from a war to secure Britain's right to sell opium, Hong Kong was reuniting with China. Harmony was being restored. But then out of nowhere, the foreign devils again assaulted the national dignity…on a soccer field. No Justice!

Now, of course, the "Handover" has come and gone. The foreign rulers are a distant memory. Hong Kong is China. The Basic Law (essentially a constitution) created Hong Kong as a Special Autonomous Region with certain personal and political freedoms that are different from the rest of China.

Now a new confrontation gives a different political context to a different soccer match. Today the side issue is not whether China owns Hong Kong. It is whether Hong Kong people are "Patriotic" and how much democracy should they be allowed to have.

The patriotism question rose earlier this year when Beijing accused Hong Kong's democracy advocates of being unpatriotic. In an attempt to settle the matter, Beijing this week issued an order declaring there would be no new democratic reforms in Hong Kong…for now. But as a conciliatory gesture, they concluded their pronouncement with the prediction that the democratic system in Hong Kong "will surely advance forward ceaselessly, and the final goal will surely be reached that Hong Kong's chief executive will be elected through universal suffrage."

Hong Kong's political expectations were extremely limited when I arrived in 1985. The colonial government had introduced very little democracy in over a century and a half, and there was none in China. But now half a million people here can peacefully march to protest a government initiative. The movement to quickly achieve full democracy is in full voice. Beijing sat back and watched these developments for a while, but when the "more democracy now" advocates went to Washington last month, the Central Government played the Patriotism Card.

This, unfortunately, spilled over into the sporting arena. Days before the big match, a sports reporter for a local paper, who should have asked Hong Kong players about their readiness to take on one of Asian football's major powers, focused instead on whether the players thought it would be unpatriotic to try to beat China and hurt their chances to make the finals. Thankfully, the players showed better judgment than the reporter. One cautious player said it would be unpatriotic to not to give China the toughest fight possible to help them prepare for the next rounds. A more assertive one said "One Country, Two Systems" is politics. In sports we are two countries, and we will do everything to win.

If all that wasn't enough, the match-up is also a classic David and Goliath sports story. China played in the last World Cup Final in Korea while Hong Kong was eliminated in the first preliminary qualifying round. China, with a population of over a billion people, has soccer players who play in the top professional leagues in Europe. Hong Kong with its seven million population has barely 100 professionals to draw from, none of whom play outside the territory. And China, patriotically, has enlisted a famous Dutchman to coach the national team, while Hong Kong's coach is home grown.

With my time in Hong Kong nearly finished, I wanted to complete the circle. I went to the match. As the near capacity crowd entered the stadium the politically correct staff gave all of us a Hong Kong and a Chinese flag. That was, however, as far as bipartisanship went. In the stands huge PRC banners waived over a noisy mainland drum corps armed with red marine flares. But nearly everywhere else only one of those little giveaway flags was flapping— Hong Kong's; and whenever the home side intercepted a pass or crossed midfield, the stands erupted.

If, like those Hong Kong players said, playing as hard as you can for your national team irrespective of the opponent is patriotism, then it was a great night for patriotism. Hong Kong played the northern giants head-to-head. Four Chinese players were stretchered off the field after clean tackles. Hong Kong's offense was aggressive throughout, and their goalkeeper defended heroically. There was nothing between the teams for more than three quarters of the game. But then, as so often happens in a tight soccer match, a ragged play near the net and a lucky touch finally put Goliath ahead for good, 1-0.

The final whistle blew and as the rest of the crowd filed out of the stadium to queue up for the buses, they left the "Two Countries" of sports and returned to the "One Country" of politics. They went home proud of their team's effort, but a little disappointed with the result.

But for me, who landed in Hong Kong just before the first match and will finally depart shortly after the second, the aggregate score was 2-2. One country, two systems, and if you wait long enough for the final goal to "surely be reached," hopefully, no loser.

[Of course, I was extremely naïve when I wrote this in 2004.]

The Final Word
A Corniche in China

There is a corniche in Qingdao, China,
Where you can stroll at the edge of the Yellow Sea.
Okay, it's not really a corniche, it's a sidewalk.
And okay, lunch is squid skewers and warm beer
Not calamari frites and Beaujolais.
But the sea smell is the same,
And in the late afternoon,
If you've been walking long, and you're tired,
You can shut your eyes, and for an instant
You will leave China for Provence.

In that instant, topless sunbathers line the beach,
And no one is spitting on the street.
The wooden fishing fleet before you
Is suddenly the Yacht Club Cannes.
And the concrete monolith behind you
Is suddenly the Hotel Carlton.
As "ni hao" fades to "bonjour," life seems serene,
And you want it to last. But its duration is brief,
Inversely related to its diversion from reality.

Be content. Do not attempt to extend the illusion,
Because the paving stones are loose
And they are difficult to see with your eyes shut.
And there is surely no harsher re-entry into China
Than a face-plant, on the sidewalk, by a squid stall,
At the edge of the Yellow Sea.

About the Author

Ken Jackson is a retired American lawyer. His employer sent him to Hong Kong in the mid 1980's and, for no apparent reason, left him there for twenty years. Over that time, he traveled throughout Asia both for work and recreation. Upon retiring, he lived in a rural village in southwestern England and in the Big Pineapple of Honolulu. From those bases, he traveled in Europe and among the Pacific islands.

His travel stories and history articles have appeared in journals and newspapers in Asia and the United States. Although he had no formal training in journalism or creative writing, he did once win a case of beer in a London newspaper's sports writing contest.

www.ingramcontent.com/pod-product-compliance
Lightning Source LLC
Chambersburg PA
CBHW021444150726
47989CB00001B/388